To

Emily Brown

SUCCESSFUL PERENNIALS

FOR THE *PENINSULA*

A Selection
by Members of
Western Horticultural Society

Foreword by Dick Dunmire
Edited by Keith Bickford
Illustrated by Christine Andrews

Published by Western Horticultural Society
Palo Alto, California

WESTERN HORTICULTURAL SOCIETY

Library of Congress Catalog Card Number 89-50197
ISBN 0-9622226-0-7

Design by Cecilia Rice Christensen

Western
Horticultural Society
P.O. Box 60507
Palo Alto, CA 94306

CONTENTS

Foreword   vii

Introduction   ix

The Perennials   1

Common Names Index   119

Contributors   125

FOREWORD

Experience is the Universal Mother of sciences.
Cervantes, *Don Quixote*

Perhaps you have noticed a certain sameness in the work of horticultural writers. Instead of the clear voices of the authors we hear the opinions of Liberty Hyde Bailey, or Miss Jekyll, or William Robinson variously paraphrased or embellished. The reason is, of course, timidity; these people were giants, and (so the reasoning goes) we must be dwarfs. Remember that these giants never contended with the problems that confront gardeners on the Peninsula — lack of winter chill, unrelenting summer drought (and often winter drought as well), to name a few; nor did they have our great advantage — a climate that gives us dominion over Kipling's palm and pine, and a great deal more.

None of the contributors to this book would claim to be a giant, but each knows some things that Bailey and the others do not, and their combined experience adds up to more years than any of them would like to think about. In this book they have graciously shared this special knowledge with those of us who, like the Music Man, don't know the territory, or are just learning it.

Dick Dunmire

INTRODUCTION

The Western Horticultural Society was founded in 1963. The membership has always been a mix of professional plantsmen and amateur gardeners, brought together by a common interest in plants and gardens. The knowledge shared at the regular meetings has been circulated in monthly bulletins as "Plant Notes". The sharing of this knowledge with gardeners outside the organization has been suggested several times over the years. In the past year an interested Publications Committee found the idea generating considerable enthusiasm. The wide-ranging plant notes were consulted, and a decision was made to concentrate on perennials, specifically those that grow well here on the San Francisco Peninsula. They will no doubt do well all around the Bay Area, but they are ones that our members have successfully grown, members who live here on the Peninsula, hence our title. We do not imply that our selection contains all the perennials that might be grown locally, but they are all successes and all plants about which we are enthusiastic. We recommend them to you.

We have striven for botanical accuracy, following, in general, *Hortus Third*. However, botanical science did not cease in 1976 when the book was published, and new micro-technology has dictated some new terminology. You will note, for instance, that some of the family names given are not the ones commonly used for a particular genus. Where a change has been made, we give the new family name first, followed by the old name in parentheses. The same is true for genetic or specific names. If you are more familiar with common names, there is an index on page 119. Some genera may be represented by a single species, in which case the heading will give genus, species, family, and then common name, if any, in that order. If more than one species is described, the main heading will list the genus, family and possibly a common name with the various species listed below in alphabetical order.

Availability of plant material was always our concern. There are fascinating plants which our members have grown but which are too difficult to find in the nursery trade for us to recommend. We have omitted them. All plants described here may not be found in all nurseries, but there are good specialty nurseries on the Peninsula that will stock the more interesting plants.

Our concern for accuracy and clarity occuped the Editorial Board for many hours. Betsy Clebsch, Elizabeth Garbett, Mary Kaye, Bart O'Brien, Marilou Vivanco, and Betty Young all made decisive contributions to the value of this book. It would not exist without them. We also benefited greatly from numerous suggestions made by Dick Dunmire. The Society is fortunate to count among its members professionals in several fields. Cecilia Christensen brought her considerable talents as a graphics designer to the layout of this book. Christine Andrews's botanical drawings delighted us all.

The contributors to the text are listed on page 125. You will hear their individual voices as they describe the plants and their experience with them. We offer you, then, accurate descriptions of those perennials that do well on the Peninsula, with personal accounts of their behavior in our gardens. We wish you good reading and good gardening.

K.B.

THE PERENNIALS

ACHILLEA. *Asteraceae. (Compositae).* YARROW. Many yarrows are grown just for cutting or for drying to use in winter arrangements, but they also make bright additions to the sunny border, where their flattened flower clusters are not only colorful but make horizontal planes that offer contrast to billowing and spiking forms. Their leaves are mostly at the base, but smaller leaves often occur along the flowering stalks, especially on the taller varieties. It is best to strip these leaves before drying the flowering stems. Yarrows can thrive with little water and are easily divided, their bloom hardly retarded by the treatment; they are deservedly popular with gardeners.

A. clavennae. This white, low-growing yarrow from the southern Alps suggests itself for use as an edging, but pools of it among other low plants are perhaps even more effective. The leaves, narrow and deeply notched, are a velvety blue gray, handsome with whiter, fuzzier woolly lamb's ears, *Stachys byzantina*, and with the gray-leaved grass, *Festuca ovina glauca*, blue fescue. Bloom is from spring into autumn.

A. filipendulina. The FERNLEAF YARROW is the best type for drying, especially the variety 'Coronation Gold' that turns to old gold as it ages. The species hails from Asia Minor and the Caucasus and is well suited to our Mediterranean climate. The leaves, rather narrow, deeply notched, rough and green, are five or more inches long, mostly basal, with successively shorter leaves along the stiff flowering stalks. The deep yellow blooms are densely clustered in flat umbels about six inches across on stems up to four feet high and are produced from spring to autumn. In a very dry garden try them in front of Matilija poppies, *Romneya coulteri*, or with light watering, behind gaillardias, especially the newer hybrids, 'Burgundy' or the more compact, low-growing 'Goblin'.

A. millefolium. MILFOIL. From Europe and western Asia, and most often white-flowered, this species is rhizomatous and can spread quickly. It has become a weed in North America, but hybridization has provided for the garden greatly improved pinkish forms with names like 'Fire King' and 'Cerise Queen'. Their leaves, dull green and softly hairy, narrow with shallow notches, are mostly basal but with smaller leaves up the flower stalks which grow to 3 ft. Flower color varies from light pink to magenta, and some very new hybrids come in cinnamon shades. The form is flattish with corymbs at most four inches across. They are poor candidates for drying as the color fades to a rather drab dusty rose, and in the garden they don't combine easily with just any flower, but for a good show try rosy shades with clumps of dark, rosy-purple penstemons, cinnamon shades with 'Blue Bedder' penstemon. To encourage lush growth, give them extra water during summer. They bloom from spring to autumn.

    A. tomentosa. This species, from Europe and Asia, can tolerate a little shade. It forms a loose mat with narrow gray-green leaves, serrated on their edges, and with its flat-topped corymbs, is almost a miniature of its bigger relations, growing no more than 10 in. tall. The golden yellow bloom is from spring into autumn. Look for pale yellow 'Primrose Beauty' or cream 'King George' to plant with the little yellow-eyed blue daisies of the so-called blue marguerite, *Felicia amelloides*.

M.V.

AJUGA reptans. *Lamiaceae. (Labiatae).* CARPET BUGLE. Ajuga is a ground cover for moist areas in sun or part shade. It sends out runners that root as they travel, so it will quickly fill an area, but if it goes too far, it isn't hard to pull free to keep it in bounds. It stays neatly only a few inches high with leaves 2 to 3 in. long and an inch wide and with smaller leaves leaves along the flowering stems. In some forms the leaves are smooth, in others wrinkled. In early summer the flowers appear in plump spikes whose height stays under 6 in. The color is usually blue, but there are forms with pink or white flowers. Improved varieties include some with dark, spinachy-green leaves and others with variegated leaves. Purplish leaves with white and pink variegation are especially popular. One with smaller leaves and flowering stems, called 'Gray Lady', has foliage with a silvery sheen and perhaps the bluest flowers of all on short spikes. Any of the ajugas is best used in quantity rather than in small patches (although I must confess to having 'Gray Lady' in a bowl with rock garden plants). I would suggest planting ajuga in curving drifts between a walkway and a lawn where its contrast in color and texture from the smooth, green grass would command some attention.

M.V.

ANDROSACE. *Primulaceae*. ROCK JASMINE.There are about 125 species, several suitable for the rock garden. The one discussed here comes from the Himalayas, is available at the better nurseries and does well in the Bay Area. As *Hortus Third* observes, the generic name is pronounced with four syllables.

A. lanuginosa. This attractive border or rock garden plant is not demanding and improves in well-being from year to year. Limp stems trail to 1 ft. arranged upon each other in a neat and decorative fashion. They are clothed with many small, silvery-hairy, ovate leaves, making a white-gray mat more than 1 ft. wide and only a few inches high. This is an evergreen ground cover but, as might be expected, the foliage looks a little bedraggled in the rainy season. The blooming season begins in spring, lasts into fall with tiny flowers in umbels about 1-1/2 in. across. They are lilac-pink with a yellow center lying face up on the mat, not numerous, but definitely noticeable. It is not difficult to dead-head those past their prime, thus improving the appearance of this generous ground cover. This species requires partial shade, especially where summers are hot. It must have perfect drainage; both air and moisture must pass freely through the medium. It does not need excessive water, but should not dry out. The stems may be cut back in late fall to control the shape of the mat, or to encourage fresh growth. It combines well with other procumbent perennials, especially those with a mat-like habit and grayish foliage, such as *Origanum dictamnus*.

E.B.

Androsace lanuginosa

Anemone x hybrida

ANEMONE. *Ranunculaceae*.

A. coronaria. POPPY FLOWERED ANEMONE is native to the Mediterranean region. Anyone who has had a bed of these bright, gloriously colored flowers, or even enjoyed someone else's planting, knows the pleasure they give. The finely divided leaves (which birds love when tender) push through the earth in early spring, followed soon by the bent flower buds. It doesn't take long for the flower stems to reach a height up to 12 in. and then the buds burst — bright red, dark purple, snowy white, and colors in between. Having given this paean, let us understand that *Anemone coronaria* tubers are not forever; they lose their vitality, or suffer from a winter that is too cold and wet. The tubers do not like cold, clammy soil. I had two years of a neighborhood show piece, then a year of occasional blooms.

In my new garden I, being slapdash, must have planted some much deeper than others, or maybe even upside down, which is quite easy to do. In any case, I did not have a lot of blooms at one time. So although I give these plants great kudos for what they give us en masse, I would like a bit more longevity and much more dependability.

A. pulsatilla. (*Pulsatilla vulgaris*). EUROPEAN PASQUE FLOWER is native from Austria to the Ukraine. This is a plant I have admired in a friend's garden, and am now growing for the first time in my new garden. It has stunning purple blossoms, opening to show golden stamens – beautiful – then it develops airy seed heads similar to those of some clematis. Where I planted it in light shade, it is lovely in August with its airy, feathery greenery. Creatures unknown ate the flowers, so I am not enjoying the feathery seed pods, but those green feathery leaves are enough for me. I will worry about the creatures next spring.

A. x hybrida. (*A. hupehensis var. japonica* x *A. vitifolia*). JAPANESE ANEMONE comes from China. Can you believe that good old Japanese anemone can have all those names? In my youth in Seattle everyone had a clump of Japanese anemones. Some people had pink, some people had a deeper rose, but the glistening white of the species was the one most admired. Who needed pink in the fall?

So let us talk of that exquisite, pure white old-fashioned Japanese anemone. It may have the fancy name of 'Honorine Jobert' or 'Alba', but really, your best bet is to get a division from one of your gardening friends. It is stoloniferous and comes up in unexpected places. Your friends will be delighted to give you a piece.

This wondrous plant likes a little shade, some water, well-drained soil, and it makes a magnificent clump of glorious green, slightly hairy, somewhat lobed leaves that send forth tall, up to 4 ft. blossoming stems. If you like pink, enjoy, but that white is something else. No prejudices here!

M.G.

ANIGOZANTHOS flavidus. *Haemodoraceae*.KANGAROOPAW comes in many colors and is used in many crosses with the other 10 species in the genus. It is usually a yellow green or rich red, but orange, pink or green can occur. The flower tube is woolly and split lengthwise with all six lobes on the same side. The tubes all tend to face the same way on their inflorescences, which makes for an extraordinary display. The stalks are 2 to 3 ft. long and the flowers keep for weeks after which they can be used in dry arrangements as they are very architectural. In my San Francisco garden the yellow form blooms 4 to 5 months and the red form all year long. Out of flower, A. flavidus makes a worthwhile foliar display with its rich, grassy mass of 20 to 40 in. leaves. Individual leaves have the sheen and soft look of extra long Douglas iris foliage. The plant wants a sunny exposure and good drainage. Propagation is easy by division or by seed, which is reputed not to require special treatment. Because of its foliage, *A. flavidus* combines well with grassy looking plants, while the statuesque quality of the flower stalks lend a strong vertical accent without blocking views of plants behind. A good ornamental that should have many uses in the garden.

T.K.

AQUILEGIA. *Ranunculaceae*. COLUMBINE. At whatever season columbines bloomed they would be welcomed for their cool, ferny foliage and graceful, colorful flowers, but coming, as they do, just as the spring bulb show is closing and before the summer perennials are in full swing, they are doubly welcome. Between the species aquilegias, many of them native to the West, and the wide variety of horticultural hybrids, there is plenty of choice for the gardener. Cultural requirements are about the same for all, full sun (in our area) or part shade, regular watering and good garden soil, rich in humus. As with most perennials, growing columbines from seed means sowing seed in the spring for bloom the following year. Quicker results can be obtained, of course, by purchasing nursery grown plants. Columbine foliage is often afflicted by mildew and a variety of other pests, but if trimmed off, a new crop will usually push up fresh and green. The four given below all bloom spring into summer.

A. caerulea. ROCKY MOUNTAIN COLUMBINE, state flower of Colorado, is perhaps the most beautiful of all the species. The sepals are light to dark blue, the petals white with long straight or spreading spurs. This species needs to be kept moist and does best in partial shade. It grows from 1 to 3 ft. tall.

A. chrysantha. Clear yellow, long-spurred flowers are borne on tall, 3-4 ft. slender but strong stems that are branched and leafy. More tolerant of sun and dryness than *A. caerulea*, reflecting its Arizona-New Mexico origins, it is persistent and hardy. The flowers are freely produced beginning in May, and one or two can still be found at the end of July. Planted among shrubs it lends a lightness and grace. This species and *A. caerulea* were among those used by hybridizers to produce the modern hybrids with tall stems and long spurs. Seed gathered fresh will germinate readily and come true to type.

A. formosa. WESTERN COLUMBINE is the short-spurred yellow and red columbine found throughout northern California. Though less spectacular than the long-spurred types, it has a special charm for

Aquilegia skinneri

those who have come upon it naturalized around springs and other damp places in the mountains. It seems especially at home in a woodsy setting with ferns, dicentra, vancouveria, etc. It grows 2-3 ft. tall.

A. hybrida. Under this name is gathered a great number of horticultural cultivars developed by crossing certain wild species to obtain a race of tall, long-spurred columbines in a wide range of colors. Almost every year brings new "improved" introductions in the seed catalogs, so that any height, habit or color seems to be available. For a tall, long-spurred form, 'McKana Giants' is very satisfactory, easy to grow from seed and has every color in the rainbow. Columbines cross very easily and self-sow readily, but the second generation of hybrid parents is usually disappointing. It is best, therefore, to cut off the stalks after they have finished blooming and try for a second crop of flowers rather than let them set seed. *E.C.G.*

A. skinneri. There are about 70 species of columbine found in the wild. *A. skinneri* from New Mexico is a choice one for the garden. Growing to 3 ft. high with glaucous, heart-shaped leaves, it produces flowers with greenish-orange petals and pale red spurs over 2 in. long. No wonder it was collected for cultivation! The flowers are elegant, but I would not call them showy. Look for bloom in mid-summer with a repeat in autumn. Growing requirements are simple: half-day sun, friable soil, moderate water, and fertilizer in springtime. Comes easily from seed. *B.C.*

ARABIS. *Brassicaceae. (Cruciferae)*. ROCK CRESS.
A. blepharophylla. COAST ROCK CRESS. This early blooming, magenta-flowered perennial comes from the coast of central California. The small, broad, dark green leaves are coarsely hairy. The flowers are an inch across and are borne on short, 6 to 12 in. spikes. If the spent flower stalks are removed, there will be rebloom. Full sun or very light shade and good drainage are primary requirements. If you try this plant away from its coastal habitat, you will need to give it some summer water.
A. breweri. BREWER'S ROCK CRESS. This earliest blooming member of the genus is often in bloom in January. The individual flowers are small and a rich, dark, rosy-purple. The most conspicuous feature of this plant is its unusual growth habit. It is a mimic of many choice alpine plants in that it forms a dense mound of tightly packed rosettes, 8 in. high and over a foot across, but unlike the alpines, it forms this dome-like cushion in less than two years. Grow it in full sun with good drainage. As its local habitat on Mount Hamilton would indicate, it needs no summer water when it is established. This plant is very attractive when used around large cobbles and boulders.

A. caucasica. (*A. albida*). One of the most useful plants for edging a walk or for the front of the border, WALL ROCK CRESS is easy to grow in almost any soil. It grows most compactly, about 6 in. tall, and flowers best where it has plenty of sun, but it will accept partial shade as well, making broad mats of soft gray-green foliage. Small spikes of white flowers cover the plant in profusion in the spring, and the foliage remains attractive throughout the year. There are single and double-flowered forms. Of the latter, 'Flore Pleno' is considered the more choice, but is not as readily available as the single. Even handsomer as an all-seasons edger is the variegated form with green leaves bordered in cream. Arabis tends to spread, though it could not be termed invasive, and a shearing back after bloom will keep it compact and confined to quarters. Snails are its worst enemy. Not only do they eat it, but it forms an ideal hiding and breeding place for them.

A. ferdinand-coburgi. This attractive variegated species is a very flat-growing plant that spreads by underground stems. It is only 3 to 4 in. high with white flowers borne on 6 to 10 in. stalks and is quite different in foliage from *A. caucasica*, the half-inch long leaves smooth rather than hairy. There is an unvariegated form as well with gray-green leaves that become greener in winter. Both of these species are easy to propagate by seed, cuttings, or division.

E.C.G.
B.O'B.

Arabis caucasica

ARENARIA montana. *Caryophyllaceae*. SANDWORT, from southern Europe, is a mat-forming plant with grayish-green leaves 1/2 to 3/4 in. long. The bright white flowers are 1 in. across with 5 broad petals around a yellowish center. They open in bright sunlight and are quite stunning in the rock garden. The plant likes a moderate amount of water, ordinary garden soil, and may be propagated by division. Bloom is in late spring. A commonly known relative is Irish moss, *A. verna*. Some plants to combine with sandwort are dianthus, origanum (especially the variegated ones), and small campanulas.

M.K.

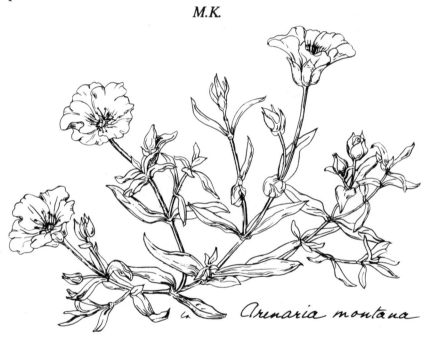

Arenaria montana

ARTEMISIA. *Asteraceae. (Compositae)*. The generic name is from Artemis, one of the names of Diana, Goddess of Hunting; more than one species was used for lightweight arrow shafts. Artemisias are grown primarily for their silvery foliage rather than their flowers. The leaves are often intricately dissected with a silky, though occasionally felted, texture. They are aromatic, some more than others, and release their fragrance best when crushed or rubbed. There are evergreen, deciduous, and herbaceous species; all require sun, soil more lean than rich, and a medium amount of water. The flowering stems often elongate and thus distort a natural, compact form; therefore, most gardeners remove these stems before they lengthen, or before the buds open in mid-summer. Artemisias are lovely in the perennial garden and can serve many purposes. They provide a wonderful contrast to the different shades of green in a garden and also help to blend and separate clashing flower colors for those of us who can't resist the warm end of the spectrum. They create a pleasing color harmony used in combination with pastel flower colors, and they look outstanding with blues of any description. Theme gardens featuring gray foliaged plants would not be complete without artemisias, and they are indispensable ingredients in a dry perennial border. An exciting feature of artemisias that Peninsula gardeners may use to advantage is the fact that they are one of the few genera that deer won't eat, and are therefore useful in native and woodland gardens where deer are abundant.

A. absinthium. WORMWOOD. This species was used to flavor the addictive liqueur, absinthe, while, as the common name suggests, the herb was also used as a purgative for worms and to alleviate stomach ailments. In the garden it can grow to be one of the largest artemisias, up to 5 ft. tall. It makes a dramatic, handsome plant where a large silvery mass or specimen is wanted, and plenty of room should be allowed so that the plant will be symmetrical. The foliage is silvery-gray, soft and silky, the leaves deeply cut. This plant is beautiful as a foil for tall purples, blues and pinks, like delphiniums and foxgloves. Because it becomes woody at the base in time, it is well to take a few cuttings each fall and replace older specimens as they pass their prime. Cuttings root easily, and the plant grows very fast. 'Silver Queen' and 'Lambrook Silver' are finer textured forms.

A. arborescens. From southern Europe comes this 1-1/2 to 3-1/2 ft. tall perennial shrub. Its yellow flowers are set against a mound of white woolly leaves which act as a noble referee between the gaudiest of flowering shrubs and perennials. Sometimes these larger artemisias are called "Dusty Miller", but as with many common names, this can refer to plants of more than one genus.

A. asoana. This lilliputian delight is from central Spain. It makes a 1 x 12 in. plus, finely textured, sterling silver mat for a scaled-down landscape, like a small rock garden, or let it spill over the edge of a trough or planter box where your and nature's handiwork is brought closer to the eye. Also, the roots will revel in the good drainage.

A. canescens. The nomenclature has been confused. This was once called *A. versicolor,* but that was a listed name only; perhaps *"A. canescens"* will fare no better. But whatever its proper name, this is one of the finest silver-foliaged plants. It makes a neat, symmetrical mound of densely branching, erect stems, covered with a filigree of curving, linear leaves. These coil and entwine, giving rise to the common name, CHAINLINK ARTEMISIA. Though not very attractive in winter, it more than earns its keep by its beautiful form from spring through fall. Propagation by cuttings is a little difficult, but the plant often roots by layering, an easier, if slower, method of propagation.

A. caucasica. Armenia is home for this tufted, carpet-forming, silvery-gray-foliaged plant. Its attributes, including its year- round good looks, are many. Requiring very little water and practically no tidying-up, it will soon creep and crawl among stepping stones or soften the front of a border. Plant in full sun with good drainage. Hardly noticeable are tiny buttons of pale yellow flowers on spikes that appear mid-summer. They are easily cleaned away by hand when dry and spent. Propagation is by division whenever needed.

A. dracunculus. TARRAGON. FRENCH TARRAGON. This species is hardly recognizable as an artemisia, for its leaves are green and not dissected. It also differs from others in that it is stoloniferous, while most of the other species grow from a single crown. It is undistinguished as a garden plant, but as a culinary herb, it is outstanding and wonderful to have available. It is herbaceous and should be cut to the ground in winter. The fresh green leaves can be harvested in spring for flavoring vinegars or marinades for chicken or fish. The leaves are easy to dry and have a milder flavor than the pungent fresh ones. Propagation is by division of a known plant. Purchased seed produces the coarser and flavorless RUSSIAN TARRAGON.

A. frigida. FRINGED WORMWOOD. This species from the mountains of North America and Siberia is somewhere between a sub-shrub and an herbaceous perennial. It is a neat grower with prostrate stems becoming as long as 20 in. The leaves are silvery, silky, hairy, 4 times pinnately cleft, making linear segments. These form into frilly rosettes that produce a charming mound. After it produces its clusters of small yellow flowers in late summer, it should be cut back hard.

A. lactiflora. Introduced in 1901 from China and India, ghost wormwood is quite unlike other artemisias described here. The foliage is dark green, and the plant builds clumps about 2 ft. across.

In August, wonderful, tall, 5 ft. stems support creamy, pale beige panicles of tiny flowers. These may be cut and dried for arrangements. Propagation is by division in winter when the foliage has died back. Full sun, friable soil, and light irrigation are all that is needed to produce good plants. For height and the ability to blend with either hot or cool colors in the border, consider this carefree artemisia.

A. pontica. Roman wormwood or small absinthe comes from central Europe and has been in gardens since the 1570's. Its medicinal qualities are valued even though it is the most delicate and least strong of the wormwoods. It is one of the ingredients in vermouth. Gardeners will favor it for its 1 ft. tall, finely cut, pewter-gray foliage that gives color throughout the growing season. Tiny, knot-like, creamy flowers appear in summer. They are hardly noticeable. Full sun, ordinary garden soil, and light irrigation are its cultural needs. It increases by underground runners, and propagation is by division in spring or summer. The foliage dies to the ground in winter. Try planting it next to red penstemons or the cardinal sage, *Salvia fulgens* to intensify their colors.

A. 'Powis Castle'. Though similar in size to *A. arborescens*, this plant is softer to hand and eye. Like a jeweler's velvet, this one makes a beautiful, luxuriant foil for flowers whose intensity or intricacy might otherwise be lost against a busier or more plebian background.

A. pycnocephala. DUNE SAGE. SANDHILL SAGE. This central California dune plant will grow in any soil and can get 2 to 3 ft. across. Its shape is somewhat loose and looks best if its small yellow infloresences are sheared off. There is a form from Pt. Reyes lighthouse called 'David's Choice', which is a perfect mound. In the garden, either brings the quality of moonlight into the daytime.

A. schmidtiana 'Silver Mound'. This variety is supposed to make a mound 12 in. tall with a spread of 25 to 30 in. Mine grows only 3 to 5 in. tall, and so may be 'Nana'. Other cultivars are 'Silver Frost' and 'Angel's Hair'. The plant's best feature is its sparkle as the early morning sunlight strikes the dew caught in its intricate foliage. The low mats or mounds created by this species are valuable in an uninterrupted drift or grown as an edging. The silvery foliage combines well with the bright colors of phlox, aubrieta, or lobelia. The strong purple of heliotrope is a wonderful contrast. The roots are rhizomatous, which makes propagation by division easy, though cuttings root readily as well. Tolerant of drought, it also responds lushly to regular summer watering. The terminal racemes of cream-colored flowers are not of much account and cause the stems to elongate and sprawl, so should be removed to keep the plant compact.

   A. stellerana. BEACH WORMWOOD, OLD WOMAN, DUSTY MILLER. From northeast Asia and eastern North America comes a relic species divided by the great ice ages. Here it does well in moist, coastal conditions. It grows to 2 ft. with an equal or larger spread, densely covered with white down. The filigree of the foliage reminds one of tooled leather. If other artemisias are "silver", then this one is best described as "platinum". The yellow flower clusters rise above the foliage in spikes. This plant deserves the front of the border.

E.B.   E.C.G.

B.C.   T.K.

C.S.

ASARUM caudatum. *Aristolochiaceae.* WILD GINGER. This beautiful, evergreen groundcover should replace ivy in the shade everywhere. Wild ginger is the best native perennial groundcover for the shade, even deep, dark shade, as long as there is accessible moisture. The red-brown flowers are an odd bell shape with long tails, but they are usually hidden by the handsome, large, heart-shaped leaves. The plants spread freely by creeping stems which are easily controlled. The plant is tolerant of most soil types (even heavy, awful clays) as long as it gets plenty of shade and water. (Do not overwater it, though; it is not a swamp or bog plant.) Grow wild ginger with other shade-loving plants, such as *Woodwardia fimbriata* or other sturdy ferns, Japanese anemones, fuchsias, or rhododendrons.

   A unique feature of this plant is that it is pollinated by slugs (very gross but unfortunately true). Snails and slugs can also ruin the lush appearance of the leaves, so you should be sure to control them by regular baiting.

   A. caudatum is native to California, where it can be found throughout the redwood belt, including our own Santa Cruz Mountains. It is very easy to propagate from cuttings or seeds.

B.O'B.

ASCLEPIAS. *Asclepiadaceae*. MILKWEED, BUTTERFLY WEED. The ancestral stock of our asclepias species came from the tropics, a fact which helps to explain the main bane of milkweed horticulture - their interminable late breaking of dormancy. Always be sure to mark or note where you have planted them or else you will very likely dig them out, damage, or kill them with a spade. Sometimes they do not sprout until May! The following three species of asclepias are host plants for the monarch butterfly caterpillars. The showy flowers attract a variety of other butterflies and insects which feed on the copious supply of nectar. Be sure to bait for snails and slugs as the new growth emerges.

    A. fascicularis. This species is our local native milkweed and can be found throughout the Bay Area, although generally not along the coast. It likes it hot and dry and will form large colonies with age. The plant grows l to 2 ft. tall and has very narrow 3 in. long, dark green to gray-green leaves. The flowers are buff-colored and are held in dense, dome-like clusters in summer. They are followed by very decorative pods and seeds. The plant is drought tolerant and easy to grow. Heavy soils are not a problem unless you overwater.

    A. speciosa. The tallest of these three species, it can reach about 3 ft. and can also form colonies by spreading underground. The leaves are about an inch or so wide, about 3 in. long and are lightly to heavily covered with a white fuzz. Balls of buff-pink, 1/2 in. flowers are produced in late summer. They are followed by the typical milkweed pods and seeds. This rugged perennial is very easy to grow in full, hot sun and is drought tolerant once it has become established. Do not overwater in summer and fall.

    A. tuberosa. Growing to 2 ft. tall, this species forms clumps rather than colonies. The foliage is rather undistinguished although it is a rich green. When in bloom the plant creates quite a spectacle. The flowers appear in summer and are vibrant shades of orange to red-orange. There are also some new selections which extend the color range more towards red and into a bright, clear yellow. Each flower is only about 1/4 in. across, but they are produced in dense head-like clusters about 6 in. across and are followed by the usual decorative milkweed pod. This plant seems to have more problems with snails and slugs than the other two.

B.O'B.

Aster x frikartii

ASTER x **frikartii**. *Asteraceae. (Compositae)*. ASTER. This hybrid between *A. thompsonii* and *A. amellus* is a great choice for people who want a "low maintenance, but colorful garden". Graham Thomas refers to this aster as "one of the six best plants which should be in every garden". This deciduous perennial produces warm, lavender-blue, daisy flowers with golden yellow centers from June to late fall, although in our area bloom can begin in May. The branching stems are slightly floppy, but usually do not require staking. The flowers are good for cutting.

Full sun is optimal, but plants will bloom nicely in dappled shade as well. Plant them 18 in. apart in good, enriched, well-drained soil with a bit of bone meal at the bottom of each hole. Spent blooms should be removed regularly, and plants should be cut back in winter when they go dormant. Propagation is by division.

Other plants with similarly colored flowers will blend well in the garden; try *Alyogyne huegelii*, *Cheiranthus 'Bowles Mauve'*, *Nepeta* x *faassenii*, and the more purple (rather than blue) form of *Solanum rantonnetii*. Lemon yellow daylily works well for contrast, as do *Coreopsis grandiflora* 'Sunray', *Oenothera berlandieri*, Shasta daisies, *Penstemon* 'Huntington Pink', *Stachys byzantina* (as an edging) and *Salvia farinacea* 'Victoria'. *A.* x *frikartii* can look striking with the soft pink flowers of Japanese anemone rising up behind it.

Plants are available at several of the better local nurseries. The improved variety 'Wonder of Staffa' is the one to look for.

D. A.

AUBRIETA deltoidea. *Brassicaceae. (Cruciferae)*. AUBRIETA. Although this is the only species of the genus commonly grown in gardens, there are other species suitable for rock gardens. This plant is really an alpine, coming from rocky cliffs and ledges of Greece, Albania, and the southern Alps. The low, spreading mat is literally covered with blue-purple flowers in spring for two or three months, after which it retires to be a modest gray-green mat. It is often combined with *Aurinia saxatile, Iberis sempervirens,* and *Phlox subulata* for a brilliant spring display. As with most alpines it likes plenty of water while it is actively growing and blooming but much less while dormant, in fact, it is then quite drought tolerant. The usual color is blue-purple, but all shades of red through blue are possible and easily obtained from a packet of mixed seed. A superior cultivar is called 'Novalis Blue', which has larger, bluer flowers and a longer blooming period than the ordinary seed-grown plants. Growing aubrieta under deciduous trees is ideal because it will have nearly full sun in the early spring, but a bit of shade in the hot summer. After blooming, the plant should be sheared by about half to keep it neat and compact.

E.C.G.

Bergenia cordifolia

BERGENIA. *Saxifragaceae*. At various times in the past bergenias have been assigned to the genera *Megasea* and *Saxifraga*, and have only recently become known as Bergenia. They have appeared prominently in such classic garden literature as Gertrude Jekyll's *Colour Schemes for the Flower Garden* (as *Megasea*) and William Robinson's *The English Flower Garden* (as *Saxifraga*). The name Bergenia commemorates the German botanist Karl August von Bergen (1704-1760).

Bergenias are extremely easy to grow, but they do deserve better treatment than most of us give them. Their needs are simple: (1) bait them for snails and slugs or these pests will quickly ruin the bold-textured foliage; (2) clean out dead leaves and spent blooming stems at least once a year; (3) divide them when they get crowded, usually after approximately 5 years. They are not particularly fussy about fertilizer, nor do they need lots of water. Light feeding and occasional watering suit them very well.

Bergenias are unparalleled as a low, bold-textured ground cover or pattern plant. They thrive in sun or shade, though full hot sun will burn the foliage, especially if the plants are drought stressed. They make a superb, lush-looking groundcover under established trees and are also effectively used with large boulders and as accent plantings. If the plants are grown in more sun than shade, the leaves of some varieties will turn a very dark reddish-purple in the coldest parts of the winter.

I find that most of the flowers are inconsequential in comparison with the foliage. The individual flowers are about the size of a nickel and are held in large clusters above the foliage. They range from white to pink to raw pink to rose to magenta and are usually single, although I have one that is semi-double. In our area they bloom from November to February, depending on species and your location.

Bergenias are well known here from two commonly encountered species, *B. crassifolia* and *B. cordifolia*. There are, however, many other very desirable species and hybrids available for our gardens. Some of the best are:

B. 'Abendglut' ('Evening Glow'). Introduced in 1950, this is a good clumping variety with nicer flowers than most in a semi-double, reddish-magenta color, though with fewer flowers per stem than the commonly grown species. 'Evening Glow' was named for the foliage, which is supposed to color very nicely in the winter, although my plants have not shown this characteristic. The clumping nature of the plant makes it unsuitable for a groundcover, but excellent in the front of a perennial border or as an accent plant.

B. 'Sunningdale'. This selection by Graham Stuart Thomas in 1954 seems to grow very well here, but is not one of my personal favorites. The leaves are not as round as I would like, but they color well in winter, a dark reddish-brown (some say like liver). This one does spread well and can be recommended as a groundcover.

B. 'Morgenrote' ('Morning Blush' or 'Morning Red'). Another German introduction from 1950, this plant has single, reddish-pink flowers and good mid-green foliage.

B. "Ed Carman's White". Beautiful, large, succulent, almost round leaves emerge a bronzy color and become a very pleasing apple green. The flowers are a good clear white, but become suffused with a reddish-pink as they age. The flower clusters are large and, at least in mine, never seem to stand upright; they always lean, giving a nice cascading effect. This bergenia has the largest rhizome and is the tallest of all I grow. It can get to be nearly 1-1/2 to 2 ft. tall. The leaves are damaged by wind and bad weather more than any other bergenia I have grown, yet I still consider it to be one of my favorites. I have not been able to find a cultivar name for this beauty, but Ed Carman has grown it for years, and so I call it "Ed Carman's White".

B.O'B.

BRUNNERA macrophylla. *Boraginaceae*. SIBERIAN BUGLOSS. Two seasons of pleasure are provided by this plant. In spring it produces sprays of delicate forget-me-not-like blue flowers above smallish leaves. Then in summer the foliage expands into handsome 3 to 6 in. wide, heart-shaped leaves that always cause comment from visitors. The plant never grows above 18 in. tall and goes dormant in winter. Once established it self-sows generously. Give it filtered shade, regular water and little else. It looks best under tall, evergreen shrubs.

K. B.

BULBINELLA floribunda.
Liliaceae. Native to South Africa, this tuberous plant forms a clump about 1 ft. wide with clear yellow flower spikes up to 2 ft. high. The individual flowers are tiny and bell-shaped. They appear in profusion on the top several inches of the stem which bends until the flowers at the top are ready to open. The leaves, basal, narrow, strap-shaped, and rather floppy, appear in winter after some rain and then die back after the blooming period.

I grow mine in full sun with no summer water, but I find that the flower spikes have been fuller and more numerous in wet winters, so additional moisture during dry winters would be beneficial. This is a showy plant requiring little care and is a cheerful addition to the winter garden, blooming in late January or February. It combines well with spring-flowering bulbs and is attractive planted near the bright, blue-flowered *Rosmarinus officinalis* 'Collingwood Ingram'.

Bulbinella may be propagated by division or from seed sown in the spring. Plants or seeds are not commonly available. Visit specialty nurseries. Seed for *B. hookeri*, a similar plant from New Zealand, is available from Thompson & Morgan.

D.D.

Bulbinella floribunda

C

CALCEOLARIA. *Scrophulariaceae*. SLIPPERWORT. We call them "Slipperworts" because of the shape of the flowers, pouchlike, as though a small doll could wear them for shoes. In the Andes you can see calceolarias growing along roadsides as you might see California poppies growing here, but in our climate these natives of Mexico and South America aren't always that easy to grow.

C. integrifolia. This species is not demanding, and its cultivar, 'Golden Nugget', might even be called obliging. It is a shrubby perennial that reaches 2 ft. or a little more. Its leaves are restful to the eye, a grayish-green, a bit rough, and shaped rather like a bay leaf. They densely clothe the plant. The flowers, appearing from spring to fall, are the sunniest of yellows, in bright contrast to the foliage. They stand in chubby bunches at the tips of the branches. The plants can take sun but may do best if shaded by larger plants. They don't need a great deal of water and seem immune to pests. For a pleasing late summer show, use them with Shasta daisies and lavender Michaelmas daisies, or you might play up their brilliancy by planting them with gloriosa daisies and gaillardias.

M.V.

CAMPANULA. *Campanulaceae*. The genus includes both herbaceous and evergreen species and which may be in three sizes, low, medium, or fairly tall. The color of the foliage is usually green, but occasionally gray. The stems frequently form spreading clumps. The flowers are either bell-shaped or star-shaped, mostly lavender-blue in color, but there are a few pink and a number of white forms. All need sun to bloom well, but should have some shade, especially in the hottest part of the day. They grow best with excellent drainage. All sizes are good in containers, and a few species which trail are best used in hanging baskets and can be planted to bloom in the fall. A few examples of the low kinds follow and many of these have trailing stems.

C. carpatica. The TUSSOCK HAREBELL is from the Carpathian Mountains. The basal leaves are small, forming a dense mound which looks something like a pincushion. The flowers are bells but they are wide and upturned instead of hanging. There are several hybrids, and many variants and cultivars; 'Dark Star', 'White Star', and 'Moonlight'. 'Blue Gem' is tiny. 'Turbinata' might be hard to find, but is to be sought for its color, very pale blue.

C. cochleariifolia, *(C. pusilla)*. Small and low, some of its cultivars are diminutive. The popular ones are 'Cambridge Blue', 'Blue

Tit' and 'Miranda', the most dwarf. The flowers of all are dangling bells. The smaller cultivars are best displayed in a rock garden or in a container. *C. elatines*, from the Italian Alps, is best known for one of its cultivars, *C.e. garganica*, (often sold as *C. garganica*). The plant grows in compact tufts with green, sharply-toothed, heart-shaped to oval leaves. Its numerous, open-petaled, blue flowers are on lateral sprays. This variety makes an excellent wall plant. Var. *fenestrellata* might be hard to find, but is choice. The plant is delicate, open, flat; the leaves are tiny. The flowers bloom on lateral stems and are distinguished by a lighter ring in the center and a prominent pistil.

C. portenschlagiana. (*C. muralis*). Bloom is in early summer. The flowers are a nice shade of lavender, but it has a superior white form 'Bavarica'. The plant is a contained spreader. The height is not much over 5 in. The leaves are small and dark green. This can be grown in a mixed planting without its scrambling out of its area too much.

C. poscharskyana. From Dalmatia comes this vigorous spreader. Its stems elongate when they trail on a slope or lean on a wall. The leaves are small and green; the numerous flowers are stars, blooming from late spring into fall. The form with lavender flowers is the better known, but a white form is also available. This species is good in a mass or as an edging, but it does look a little messy to the gardener who likes plants trim and neat.

There are many more of these delightful low-growing species. I have chosen a few which I have grown in my mid-Peninsula garden, providing them with some moisture, some shade, some fertilizer. There is a group of campanulas of intermediate height, but since I have no favorites here, I will jump to the upright group, those having erect stems 2 or more feet tall. In this range there are several kinds excellent for borders or cutting gardens. I have chosen only a few to describe and these because of good behavior or generous bloom. Flowers are cup-shaped or bell-shaped, arranged on erect stems from a basal clump in most cases evergreen. The persistent rosette may be renewed by grooming. The seasons of bloom are summer and fall.

C. glomerata. The purple or white flowers are produced in crowded globular heads. The leaves are narrowly heart-shaped. They form a persistent basal mat from which the flowering stems grow to as much as 3 ft. but usually less. These multiply from spring into fall making a dense colony. 'Joan Elliot' is a form selected for improved habit and finer flowers; these are more bell-shaped than the funnel shape of the species. Var. 'Dahurica' is vibrant purple. 'Sneekrone' is a good white and its vase life is particularly long.

C. lactiflora. This is one of several taller species, growing to 6 ft. and needing to be staked. Clumps spread to more than 2 ft. wide with branching stems. The flowers are broad and bell-shaped, with color closer to pale blue than lavender. This is a sturdy species to combine with shrubs or subshrubs and goes very well with roses because of its blending color. If this species is not common in the nurseries, it may be shared by division.

C. persicifolia. This peach-leafed campanula has nodding, cup-shaped flowers on erect stems. The white cultivar 'Alba' is used as often as the more typical lavender. The tall slender stems vary in height but are self-supporting. Good cultivars such as 'Fleur de Neige' and 'Moerheimii' should be sought, as well as modern introductions. Give them part shade, and look for their bloom in summer.

C. primulifolia. This species is from Spain and Portugal. It grows to 3 ft. tall and has a rough leaf texture as opposed to the smooth texture of *C. persicifolia*. New leaves are thought to look like primrose leaves, as the species name would suggest. The number of flowering stems increases each year as the clumps expand. The inflorescences are narrow, branched, with numerous, broadly bell-shaped, soft lavender flowers, up to 2 in. across. Bloom is late summer into fall. The species often seeds itself, but not so prolifically as to become a nuisance. It may be grown from seed or increased by division. Less sun is required for bloom than in any other campanula.

E.B.

Campanula primulifolia

CENTAUREA cineraria. *Asteraceae. (Compositae)*. DUSTY MILLER. This is only one of several plants commonly referred to as "Dusty Miller". *C. maritima, C. gymnocarpa, Cineraria maritima, Senecio cineraria* are others. All of them have white, velvety foliage, as the common name would suggest. This one forms a clump of 1 ft. long, deeply pinnately lobed leaves. The flowers are 1 in. across, borne singly on stems above the foliage, and are usually purple, though occasionally yellow. Bees love them. Cut them back after blooming. The plants divide easily and fill in quickly from the smallest division. Any soil will do, but they need full sun and not much water. They are fairly drought tolerant.

B.Y.

CERASTIUM tomentosum. *Caryophyllaceae*. SNOW-IN-SUMMER. The common name derives from the sheets of white flowers that cover the plant in late spring and early summer. It is probably the only species of this genus that we know here. It came to us from Italy and Sicily, so you can see it should be well suited to our so-called Mediterranean climate. And well suited it is, thriving in hot sun without a drop of water for months on end. It can endure just a little shade, but will be spindly and weak in too much shade. This is a little mat-forming plant that reaches only around 6 in. in height, but can make a big pool several feet across fairly quickly. Its leaves are a light gray-green, silvery on the reverse, only an inch long and less than half as wide, and as velvety as a horse's muzzle. The little flowers are surprisingly showy with flaring, notched petals standing on branched stems just barely above the foliage. When the blossoming comes to an end, the plants should be sheared with hedge clippers to tidy them up, and this is a good time to do any shaping to keep them in bounds. You can use some of the trimmings to start new plants. 'Silver Carpet' is a cultivar that has become available lately in most nurseries. It has leaves half as long as the species, giving it a denser, more compact appearance. More dainty, I think. Its flowers are not noticeably different, but for me it is only a shy bloomer, and I wish it would have more flowers. I grow snow-in-summer with small, blue-flowered bulbs – grape hyacinth, scillas, and that old-fashioned little relative of onions that goes by the ponderous name, *Ipheion uniflorum*, spring star flower.

M.V.

CHRYSANTHEMUM. *Asteraceae. (Compositae)*. There are several chrysanthemums besides the familiar florists' chrysanthemum, *C. morifolium*. The special requirements of that species make it a less likely choice for the perennial border, and it will not be treated here. Two of the other species, however, are good choices for our gardens.

C. haradjanii. (*Tanacetum haradjanii*). This is a useful gray-white sub-shrub growing from 1/2 to 1-1/2 ft. tall. The finely dissected, fern-like foliage makes it an interesting ground cover or border accent plant. It is fairly drought tolerant and will, in fact, get root rot (*Phytophthora*) rather easily with too much water. Give it a well-drained soil. As plants age and start to die back at the base, cut them back and they will sprout anew. Divide them every 2 or 3 years in the spring to keep them compact. Propagation is by cuttings or divisions. Cuttings should be kept on the dry side to prevent rot.

C. maximum. (**C. superbum**). SHASTA DAISY. This is the common but useful large-flowered white daisy developed by Luther Burbank. Growing 1 to 3 ft. in any sunny garden soil, it is handy in the border as an accent or a filler. It can go longer than most without water, but needs a thorough soaking when in bloom. The large, single, double or fringed blossoms last a long time as cut flowers. The plants are attractive to slugs, snails, and gophers, all pests we have come to know. Propagation is easy from seed in early spring, cuttings in June or July and divisions in fall or winter. There are a number of varieties available. I am familiar with and like the following varieties. 'Esther Read', an old favorite that produces large, double, white flowers on stems to 2 ft. tall from June to frost; 'Mayfield Giant' has large off-white flowers on stems up to 3-1/2 ft. and under good conditions can be invasive; 'Snow Lady' has large flowers with frilly centers. It is quick to perform — start seed indoors in February, plant out the first of June, and enjoy the blooms from late July or August until frost. Its stems are shorter, only 1 ft. tall. 'Roggli Super Giant' has large single blooms, great as cut flowers.

B.Y.

COREOPSIS verticillata. *Asteraceae. (Compositae)*. One of the charms of this coreopsis species from the eastern United States is its difference from others in the genus. People will often argue that it can't possibly be a coreopsis, its growth habit is so different from the more commonly grown *C. grandiflora* and *C. lanceolata. C. verticillata* grows in a neat clump up to 2 ft. tall and about 1 ft. wide. Its stems are covered with needle-like leaves, and those same stems carry many star-like yellow flowers throughout the summer. It is extremely tolerant of drought and seems to prefer soil that is not too rich. In my experience it goes completely dormant in the fall, but after the first rains I find new starts in quite an area surrounding the original plant. These are shoots arising from spreading rhizomes.

The variety 'Moonbeam' is described in the *Wayside Garden Catalog*, Fall, 1988: "We rate this as one of the 10 all-time great perennials ... has delicate, creamy flowers profusely produced throughout the entire summer." It could well be a much easier plant to use in the garden than its yellow-yellow cousins.

M.G.

Coreopsis verticillata

CUPHEA hyssopifolia. *Lythraceae*. FALSE HEATHER. Most cupheas come from Mexico and Central America and are too tender for our climate except as houseplants. This species, though tender, does fairly well here. My garden is in a cold pocket and the plants will often be top-killed in a severe winter, but they always come back; the frost only ensures that I prune them each year.

The plant is really a shrublet with a woody trunk and branches, never growing over 2 ft. tall and usually less with pruning. The leaves are small and heather-like, hence the common name. The tiny flowers cover the plant for a long period in summer and may be white, purplish, or magenta. If you have plants of more than one color, seedlings will appear (profusely) showing a mix of both parents. The plants look well with other small-leaved shrubs such as *Daphne collina*.

K.B.

DELPHINIUM. *Ranunculaceae*. PERENNIAL LARKSPUR. This statuesque beauty is the perfect late spring to fall accent in pink to blue to purple. It is good for the rear of the perennial border or as a complete bed in the background of a large garden. Tall flower spikes containing hundreds of 1 to 2 in. flowers arise from a central crown of deeply lobed, almost fern-like leaves.

D. elatum. CANDLE LARKSPUR. In cultivation for over 400 years, this species from Central Europe to Siberia needs a mostly sunny, rich, well-drained soil. Virtually all varieties must be staked or the tall flower stalks will fall over. Mice, slugs, and snails love delphiniums, so precautions must be taken. They are also susceptible to rust and mildew; watering at the base, not overhead, helps. But one should not be dismayed by the difficulties, for these gorgeous, tall candles in many shades of blue, pink, and white are well worth the effort. After the first bloom, trim off the top of the flower stalks and you will be rewarded by a second, smaller bloom in the fall from axillary buds. The blossoms do not last long as cut flowers (2 to 3 days) but are majestic while they do. They also do well as dried flowers. Just cut the flower stalks and hang them in small bunches in a dark, warm, dry place for 2 to 3 weeks. Individual flowers can be used in potpourri or on botanical wreaths.

The varieties most often grown, and so the ones most available, are the Pacific Coast Hybrids . These grow to 8 ft. tall with colors from pink to purple but mostly blue flowers. The seeds can be collected and will come true. Blue Fountains is similar to the Pacific Coast Hybrids, but is shorter, to about 4 ft. tall, and comes in all shades of blue. Buy new seed; garden collected seed probably won't come true. Magic Fountains is shorter than the others, usually less than 3 ft. and so may not need staking. Flower sprays are thicker, with slightly larger flowers in pink to blue to purple.

All varieties grow easily from seed. If you get frost in your area, start seed in March to April indoors. When transplanting seedlings be sure not to cover the growing point at the center of the crown; they will rot easily if covered. Plant out in May for July to October bloom the first year. If you do not get frost, start seeds in late summer. Plant out in October to overwinter and get bloom in late spring through fall. All varieties need rich, well-drained soil and regular feeding. Cuttings can also be taken from summer side growth. After the first year, they can be propagated by division in the fall.

B.Y.

There are also many native California delphiniums, though only a few have been cultivated. The two that have received the most attention, *D. cardinale* and *D. nudicaule*, are unlike the popular *D. elatum* in that they have orange to red flowers. They are also a favorite of hummingbirds. The cultural requirements of the natives are also different. All should have ample water during their growing season in the spring and should then be allowed to dry out in the summer when they are dormant. They will re-appear, if they survive, shortly after the first winter rains, usually sometime in November. They are not long lived in the garden but are worth replacing if necessary.

D. cardinale. This large, easy-to-grow garden subject attains a height of 5 ft. and blooms in June. Its flowers are scarlet and yellow, over 1/2 in. across and are held closely to the central stalk. In the wild this plant is found from Monterey County through southern California in clearings and in chaparral. Full sun and good drainage are the keys to success with this plant, although it will grow in partial shade. In order to make any sort of color splash, you will need six or more plants as they have a very wispy appearance and a single specimen is easily lost in a flower garden.

D. nudicaule. These are found in our local region on fairly steep, rocky slopes with a northern or eastern aspect. The plant is 1 to 2-1/2 ft. tall with many 1/2 in. red flowers. Flower and individual flower stalk size decrease as they approach the tip of the flower stalk. This is an excellent choice for a sunny rock garden or a partially shaded border which has good drainage. In our area bloom is in April and May.

D. variegatum. This plant is 1 to 2 ft. tall and blooms in early spring. Its flowers are a deep violet-blue, up to 1-1/2 in. across. It seems to be a bit longer lived if it is allowed to dry out in the summer.

B.O'B.

DIANTHUS. *Caryophyllaceae*. The best known members of the genus are probably the florists' carnations, but being floppy plants that require special methods to keep them upright, these are miserable garden flowers. Some of the low-growing pinks, however, are delightfully easy in home gardens. They need fairly rich soil, enriched with lime if the soil is acid, sunshine, and not too much water. They will need regular cutting of spent blooms and a sharp lookout for slugs and snails, which like to nibble the outer layer of the flowering stems. None of this is hard to do, and while you are tending the plants, you can enjoy their bright flowers. Plants are easily started from seed sown in the spring. They will germinate in flats within a week to ten days, and then can be potted up into four-inch pots to be grown on until set out in the garden for bloom the following spring.

D. deltoides. MAIDEN PINK. This European species forms a mat of tiny, dark green leaves spreading slowly outward. On short, wiry stems little miniature, carmine-colored, single pinks, less than a half inch across, stand above the mats, blooming spring through autumn. They seed generously and can spread where least expected in the garden, but what a charming little intruder it is! 'Brilliancy' is a taller and darker, almost fluorescent, pinkish red cultivar that forms loose clumps about eight inches across with flowers a little larger than the species, one or several on a stem, standing no more than a foot high. It makes a colorful edge in front of *Felicia amelloides*, and looks tidily bright with the white form of the felicia. 'Microchip' is a recently introduced cultivar that produces masses of little blossoms in white or shades of rose with eye rings. As cut flowers they can be used in tiny arrangements on a window sill above the kitchen sink or on a desk where you can enjoy them close-up. In the garden clumps reach about 8 in. across and 15 in. high.

D. knappii. This species from Yugoslavia is very different from others in the genus. It makes a rounded clump of dark green leaves with sturdy 15 in. flowering stalks that have dense clusters of little, pale yellow flowers at the tip. The florets don't bloom all at once, so each cluster will include buds, flowers, and browned, spent flowers from spring through autumn. It is less showy than most pinks, but it is dainty as a border or in masses to conceal the old foliage of dwarf German iris.

M.V.

Diascia rigescens

DIASCIA. *Scrophulariaceae*. The genus *Diascia* has quickly become a smash hit at garden centers in the Bay Area in recent years due to the fact that they are quite charming, colorful plants. Diascias are related to snapdragons, fox-gloves, the native galvesia, penstemons, mulleins, and veronicas, to name just a few. About 21 species of *Diascia* are considered perennial out of around 50 total, all originating in South Africa. Presently the following perennial species are the most commonly available in our local nursery trade, although, with some searching, others may be found in nurseries specializing in unusual plants.

D. barberae. TWINSPUR. According to *Hortus Third*, this is an annual species, but Kim Steiner, curator of the Kirstenbosch Arboretum in South Africa, informs us that what we call 'Ruby Field ' is actually the species *barberae* and is always perennial. The flowers are a rich coral color. The plant is compact, 8 to 10 in. in height including flower spikes. It is stoloniferous and so may spread in the garden, but it is not invasive and can be effective meandering through a rock wall.

D. fetcaniensis. *(D. feltonii)*. This is a more lanky species. It reaches 8 to 10 in. in height by 2 ft. wide and is of a lighter shade than 'Ruby Field'.

D. rigescens. This seems to be the largest of the species available locally, reaching 18 in. in height and 2 to 3 ft. in width. It also has the largest flower spikes of them all in a deep, peach-pink color.

D. vigilis. Even looser growing than *D. fetcaniensis*, this species will mound up 12 to 18 in. high and 2 ft. wide. It is the lightest shade of soft apricot and blends well with other pastel colors in the border.

I have grown these species in full sun and believe that is what they prefer as they tend to get leggy and bloom less profusely in the shade, although 'Ruby Field' will tolerate light shade and still bloom well. They all bloom in summer, although *D. rigescens* seems to want to bloom all at once in late spring to early summer, while the others will continue to bloom throughout the warmer months if deadheading is done regularly. If plants build up a thatch, it is good to do some cutting back to rejuvenate them, and they respond quite well to this treatment. The diascias do best under our coastal conditions in the Bay Area and they dislike the hot, dry, Central Valley climate. Well-drained soil is preferred, and plants may succumb to fungus if constantly wet.

In general, diascias perform better in the garden if new plants are started each year and planted in the spring, which is neither difficult nor expensive to do since they propagate easily from cuttings taken from soft new growth just about any time of the year.

C.S.

DICENTRA. *Fumariaceae*. BLEEDING HEART. The name "dicentra" is from the Greek, meaning twice spurred, referring to the two points hanging from the flowers. This is an exquisite group of clump-forming to spreading species with pendulous heart-shaped flowers and finely dissected, fern-like leaves. All are good as cut flowers.

D. chrysantha. GOLDEN EARDROPS. This California native is found on the eastern side of the Coast Ranges from Mendocino south to Baja and in the Sierra foothills south from Calaveras County. Unlike the other species, it likes dry, sunny places and grows best in poor, rocky soil. It is also more erect than other dicentras, growing to 4 ft. Leaves are blue-gray and basal. The flowers are heart-shaped, the color of pure gold, and extremely fragrant. They are held in arching showers above the leaves and look great in the middle or back of a sunny border needing a yellow accent. Bloom is in late spring. This dicentra mixes well with *Salvia, Penstemon,* or *Eriogonum*. It has a deep taproot, so it doesn't transplant easily. Sow seed in peat pots 3 or 4 to a pot (germination is always poor), and plant out without disturbing roots, or sow seed in place in the garden. In the wild, seed apparently germinates best after fire, so after sowing seed, spread a thin layer of straw over flat or peat pots, and burn it off. (Don't do this in the living room.)

D. eximia. FRINGED BLEEDING HEART. Native to the east coast of the U.S., this species is similar to *D. formosa*, but the leaves are a paler green and it is not so aggressive, needing to be divided only every three or four years. The flowers are deep mauve to rose-pink with partially reflexed spurs. Bloom is from May to August and will be better with some sun. Root rot is a serious problem unless the soil is well-drained. 'Clay's Variety' has bright pink racemes all summer and sets no seed. Foliage lasts in the heat.

D. formosa. WESTERN BLEEDING HEART is a California native found in the redwood forests, damp, shaded woodlands of the Coast Range, and along stream beds in the Sierras. It needs a rich, well-drained, moist soil; root rot can be a problem. It spreads rapidly from underground stems and makes a nice ground cover under trees. It is also good in a shady rock garden and can be divided yearly if it needs to be confined. The plants grow to 18 in. tall with bluish-green, deeply-divided, fern-like leaves. The flowers are pink to rose to red-tinted purple, and bloom May to September. 'Bountiful' has large, deep pink to plum flowers in spring and again in autumn. 'Sweetheart' is a pure white form that shines in a night moon garden. 'Adrian Bloom' has grayer leaves, crimson flowers, and will take more sun. 'Paramount' is similar but darker. 'Alba' has paler leaves and white flowers in small bunches; there is a question whether this is *D. eximia* or *D. formosa*. 'Silversmith', a newer variety, may be more hardy than 'Alba'. *D. f. oregana*, native to the Siskiyous, grows to only 8 in. tall. The flowers are cream-colored with pink tipped petals. Propagate *D. formosa* from seed, by root sections cut off and planted in winter, or by division in spring.

D. spectabile. COMMON BLEEDING HEART, LADY-IN-A-BATH is the classic bleeding heart, native to Japan, Korea, and China. (To see the lady, turn the fully opened flower upside down and pull open the petals.) The flowers, rosy-red with white tips, appear in late spring dangling gracefully from arching stems. There is also a form with white flowers. The leaves are larger and coarser than those of other dicentras, and they die down and disappear in late summer. The plant forms a clump and needs dividing only every 3 to 5 years.

B.Y.

DIGITALIS x **mertonensis**. *Scrophulariaceae*. FOXGLOVE. This is a hybrid between *D. grandiflora* and *D. purpurea*, but comes true from seed. When grown in half-day sun, this foxglove will develop 3 ft. spikes of raspberry pink flowers above a rosette of deep green leaves. It is a true, but not a long-lived perennial, and it does make a clump that can be divided. One flower spike left to seed will provide more than enough transplants in the spring. Our familiar foxglove, *D. purpurea*, is a biennial, and so is not included here.

E.C.

DODECATHEON clevelandii ssp. insulare. *Primulaceae*. ISLAND SHOOTING STAR. Far and away the easiest of the genus to cultivate, the exciting and beautiful island shooting star is also the largest, with basal rosettes nearly 12 in. across, and flower stems about 18 in. high. The gracefully nodding, cyclamen-like flowers are a bright magenta-pink and are nicely set off by their bronzy stems. The pale, gray-green, fleshy leaves emerge shortly after the first rains in the fall, (just when I'm sure that I had neglected it too much the previous summer and resolutely promise to do better with my next plant. This has been happening for the past eight years now, and I still have the original plant, so you know it can take abuse).

The plant can get by on rainfall alone, although during very dry winter and spring periods it should be watered. I have grown the shooting star in part shade to nearly full sun, and it always performs well. I find the key to success is not to baby this fragile-looking plant, especially after it goes dormant. I grow mine in a container, and when it does die down, I move it to a shady spot so it won't desiccate so quickly in the summer. If it is lucky, my plant may get two or three brief waterings in the summer, just enough to keep it alive.

Aphids seem to attack the plant just as the leaves start to yellow and the flowers have gone to seed. I always take this as a cue to cut off the flower stalks and reduce watering until the plant disappears in June and I'm sure it is dead again. There are many other species of dodecatheon, but none of them is as easy to grow as the island shooting star.

B.O'B.

ECHINOPS exaltatus. *Asteraceae. (Compositae).* GLOBE THISTLE. Native to the Mediterranean and central Asia, this member of the thistle family does very well in our Peninsula climate, but is probably more often seen in English and eastern U.S. gardens where summers are wetter than ours. For it to do its best here, it should have an occasional drink, especially from midsummer to late fall, when it blooms. The flower heads are composed of individual blossoms clustered together to form perfectly round, blue lollipops 2 in. across on long stems. They are prized by flower arrangers who use them either fresh or dry. To dry them, the stems must be cut while the blossoms are in bud; once the spiky buds have opened into little blue stars, they will fall off as they dry. The plant is usually described as "coarse", and certainly it isn't dainty. The clumps may reach as much as 3 or 4 ft. in height and almost as much in width. They are deep-rooted and may be hard to remove from the wrong spot in the garden. The leaves are a little prickly but can be handled without gloves. They are a dull, dark, grayish-green, large and deeply cut, something like those of *Acanthus mollis*, except that they are less rigid and glossy. The flowers are produced from midsummer to late fall, and after blooming stops, the foliage should be cleaned away right to the ground. When new growth appears in the spring, you can propagate new starts by digging them from the edges of the clumps. To enjoy globe thistle in the garden, plant it behind pink or white phlox, Shasta daisies, or golden-flowered gloriosa daisies.

M.V.

EPIMEDIUM. *Berberidaceae.* Native to temperate Europe and Asia, there are a number of species and varieties in cultivation, all of them low growing, and several will spread to make wide drifts in the shade, 10 to 15 ft. in a few years. The leaves create an airy effect, soft green, or green with bronze highlights. The clumps may be sheared for total renewal or each older stem may be cut out separately. All kinds can be used as a low undercover for shrubs or along woodland paths. They combine very well with *Vancouveria, Tiarella, Asarum, Disporum, Uvularia,* the more dwarf ferns, and the very dwarf bulbous plants like *Lapeirousia.* The new leaves of *Epimedium* are very delicate in texture, so to provide some contrast, *Brunnera* and *Omphalodes,* or even *Cornus canadensis,* if the soil is sufficiently fibrous, can be planted nearby.

Epimedium does best in cool situations with friable, damp soil. It is tolerant, however, once established and the rhizomes are energetic, thriving even among the roots of trees if these are not too compacted. Flowers are in dainty sprays, cream- colored, yellow, pink, and apricot. Some flowers have spurs, some do not. Bloom is mostly in early spring, but blossoms stay fresh a long time. The flower is sometimes called "inside-out-flower" because the petals are so strongly recurved, while the pistil and stamens point sharply in the opposite direction.

A number of species do well on the Peninsula, but only a few are described here. They are available in specialty nurseries, or one can have plants sent from nurseries in the Northwest. There are hybrids and named cultivars. Propagation is by division in spring or fall.

E. alpinum. This species is from northern Italy to Albania. It is noted for its delicate, heart-shaped leaves. They are pale green, flushed copper-red when young. It is especially important to cut out the older leaf sprays so that the new growth is more visible.

E. grandiflorum. BISHOP'S HAT is from Japan and Manchuria. The leaves have 5 to 9 leaflets with heart-shaped bases, becoming ovate-triangular with spiny edges. The flowers are 1 to 2 in. wide, long-spurred, and resemble a bishop's hat, as the common name would suggest. Several color combinations are available in various cultivars, most carrying the name "Queen". The cultivars have been crossed with *E. pinnatum* or its varieties.

E. pinnatum ssp. colchicum. This species and its varieties have been used as parents in hybridizing. The flowers are smaller than *E. grandiflorum*, but are a bright yellow, some with short, red spurs. The leaves turn red to bronze in the fall, probably giving the best color of any described here.

E.B.

ERIGERON. *Asteraceae. (Compositae)*. FLEABANE. The members of this genus are referred to as fleabane, which doesn't begin to tell the full story of its immunity to garden pests. They are all easy to grow and require little water, both qualities we should welcome.

E. glaucus. SEASIDE DAISY, BEACH DAISY. This California native will reward you with many lavender to purple daisies at intervals from spring through fall. It will tolerate most soil conditions, even heavy clay, as long as it is not overwatered. It is, however, longer lived in well-drained conditions where it will not get overheated in summer. Full sun suits it best; light shade is tolerable. In its usual forms, this plant can grow up to 2 ft. tall and have large, coarse foliage in shades of blue-gray green. There are several selections available in our area; two of my favorites are:

E. g. 'Cape Sebastian'. From southern Oregon, this selection is an exceptional, prolific, compact, dwarf form with long, pale lavender ray florets. The plant reaches 4 to 6 in. high and can spread up to 2 or 3 ft. wide. The bright green leaves are a broad oval shape and are less than 1-1/2 in. long. The individual flower heads are the size of a fifty-cent piece. Try it in containers mixed with other coastal natives such as *Camissonia cheiranthifolia, Erioganum latifolium*, and low, native, annual flowers.

Erigeron karvinskianus

E. g. 'W.R.' This form is also low-growing. The foliage mat will reach 6 to 10 in. in height and will quickly form a lush mat 3 ft. or so wide. The long, narrow, dark green leaves are 3 to 6 in. long. The flowers are borne in lax clusters and appear throughout the year. The name 'W.R.' honors Wayne Roderick, a well-known, expert plantsman and promoter of our native flora.

E. karvinskianus. FLEABANE does best in a sandy soil, though is not fussy about this, and produces broad, 18 in. tall mounds of bloom from spring to fall. The daisy-like flowers are 3/4 in. across with white or pink ray flowers in a double row around a bright yellow center. The cultivar 'Mairei' has larger and darker flowers. The leaves are small and thin and are hardly noticed when the plant is in full bloom. Give it sunshine or light shade, and use it as a transition plant next to walks, steps or walls. It fills the gaps in your carefully planned landscape and gives it a casual look.

A native of Mexico, this plant will grow easily from seed, (blooming the first year), division, or cuttings (get some from a friend). Some think it is invasive, but I've found it easy to control, perhaps because I'm always checking. Good plants to accompany it are cottage garden plants such as penstemon, lavenders, or salvias in the dark purple range.

M.K.
B.O'B.

ERIOGONUM. *Polygonaceae.*

E. grande rubescens. RED BUCKWHEAT is native to the Channel Islands off Santa Barbara. This is a woody plant whose branches lie on the ground and have upright tips about 1 ft. high. Flower stalks appear from the tips and are 1 to 2 ft. long, leaning toward the sun. The plant spreads to around 2 ft. The flowers are in clusters and are a dusky-rose color. The 1 to 3 in. long leaves are gray-green above and woolly white below. Plants bloom from May to September, and if the flower clusters are left on, seeds will drop and, given rain at the appropriate time, seedlings will appear. The unusual rose color of the flowers combines well with the color of the foliage and makes this easy-to-grow, drought tolerant plant a useful one for sunny, dry gardens. No summer water is necessary. Plants come readily from seed and are also available from most native plant nurseries. In my garden I have this eriogonum massed with *Limonium perezii, Lantana montevidensis*, and *Zauschneria californica*, a combination I enjoy.

    E. crocatum. SAFFRON BUCKWHEAT is native to Ventura County, California. This low, compact plant, up to 18 in. tall, spreads to around 4 ft. The stems are white and woody, and the 1 to 1-1/2 in. leaves are almost white. The sulphur-yellow flowers appear in rounded clusters from April to August or September and become rust-colored as they age. This plant requires good drainage and little or no summer water. It is a good plant for a dry slope, but is not suitable for a manicured garden as it becomes rather woody with age. Propagation is by seed, and plants are available at most native plant nurseries. It combines well with other gray-foliaged plants such as artemisias, helichrysums, and lavenders.

D.D.

ERODIUM. *Geraniaceae*. HERON'S BILL. These plants are commonly known as heron's bill or crane's bill because of the form of the seed capsule. Most are native to the Mediterranean region and prefer a dry, sunny location with loamy soil. The foliage grows in basal tufts, and the flowers are delicate and interesting in detail. They do not object to being transplanted, therefore make good candidates for sharing with your neighbors. Propagation is by seed or division. *Hortus Third* says that some are used for forage crops in California and some have become weeds. The ones described here belong to neither group.

    E. chamaedryoides. ALPINE GERANIUM. Originally from Majorca, this is a dark green, mat-forming plant with small, toothed leaves and white flowers with pink veins. However, the variety most commonly seen is 'Roseum', which has pink flowers with darker pink veins. There is also a double form and one with somewhat larger, deeper pink flowers. 'Roseum' grows about 2 to 3 in. tall and spreads to about 6 to 12 in. Growth is slow to moderate. It blooms from spring to fall. This little delicacy prefers regular moisture and looks more lush with a little shade. It is particularly good as an edging or between stepping-stones and in rock crevices.

    E. chrysanthum. The foliage on this one is finely divided and a lovely soft gray-green. It grows 6 in. tall by about 15 in. wide. The pale yellow flowers are held above the leaves in loose clusters of 2 to 6. It blooms in spring, summer, and into fall, a few flowers at a time, but the foliage always looks handsome. It is good in a perennial border or rock garden, especially with blue-flowering plants such as *Salvia patens*, *Phlox subulata*, *Geranium himalayense*, and *Agapanthus* 'Peter Pan'. This plant is rather hard to find, so call some nurseries before you make a long trip.

E. guttatum. This is a welcome addition to our gardens, because it blooms so profusely. It spreads, but is not invasive. The leaves are medium green, dissected, and feathery. The flowers, blooming from spring through fall, are held above the plant on 6 to 8 in. stems and are white with a maroon spot at the base of the two uppermost petals. A native of southwestern Europe, this plant should be used where its small scale can be appreciated and easily seen, as in a stone sink or container garden. A low-growing, gray-foliaged plant would be a good accompaniment. There is some confusion in the various descriptions of this plant. Ingwersen's *Manual of Alpine Plants* describes it as I have here, and it fits the description of the plant I recently purchased at Western Hills Nursery, but *Hortus Third* gives an entirely different description of the flower.

E. hybridum. Under this name is sold a distinctive plant with finely cut, gray foliage about 8 in. tall and pale pink flowers. It grows in practically full sun. You will find it is nice with *Rosa* 'Pink Pet'. It is well-behaved and blooms almost all summer.

M.K.
B.C.

Erodium chrysanthum

ERYNGIUM paniculatum. *Apiaceae. (Umbelliferae)*. Eryngiums are very easy garden subjects. There are innumerable species to try, and taxonomically they are in a state of total confusion. Nearly all are drought tolerant perennials, and most of the better species for the garden prefer good drainage and/or sandy soil. All eryngiums are thistle-like, spiny plants and many species have a steely, metallic sheen about the spiny bracts which grow beneath the insignificant flowers clustered into dense, thimble-like domes. *E. paniculatum* is one of my favorites because it is such an odd plant. Its spiny, narrow leaves form a rosette from 1 to 2 ft. across. The "spines" are very long and hair-like, and, although they look fierce, they are actually quite soft on green foliage, (watch out for the dried foliage!). There are many 1 in. thimbles of flowers scattered on stems of various lengths along the central stalk which can reach a 3 ft. height. The flowering of this plant is of structural interest rather than a thing of great beauty.

B.O'B.

ERYSIMUM. *Brassicaceae. (Cruciferae)*. WALLFLOWER. There is much confusion about the two genera that contain the wallflowers. *Erysimum* is distinguished botanically from *Cheiranthus* by the presence of median as well as lateral nectar glands at the base of the stamens, a character that few of us are going to be able to discern at a glance. *Hortus Third* labels the old garden favorite, the ENGLISH WALL FLOWER, *Cheiranthus cheiri*. Here we will describe only those wallflowers *Hortus* places in the *Erysimum* genus, knowing full well that nursery labels may follow some other system.

E. 'Bowles' Mauve'. If there were an honors list of the ten best perennials, 'Bowles' Mauve' would be sure to be on it. The long-lasting flowers are a clear, soft purple ("mauve" to the British) against blue-green foliage. It has a neat mounding habit, grows some 2 ft. tall, is undemanding as to soil and water and has a good resistance to pests and diseases. This plant has it all. In full sun it is one of the first perennials to bloom in the spring. By July the old flower stalks should be removed and more will be produced for the remainder of the year; in fact, it is seldom out of bloom. Because this is a sterile hybrid, no seeds are produced, so propagation must be by cuttings.

E. hieraciifolium. SIBERIAN
WALLFLOWER. This species has an erect
and branching habit, growing to 18 in.
with clear orange or yellow flowers in
rounded heads. The plants are resistant to cold and disease, but good
drainage is a must. Perennial, they will
persist for years with little care. They
tolerate summer dryness very well; in
fact, the common name derives from
their readiness to seed themselves into
old stone walls and persist without fur-
ther attention. Here on the Peninsula
sow seed in early fall for bloom the following spring.

E. 'Jubilee Gold'. The flowers
completely cover this low-growing mat
in spring, making a pool of gold in the
front of the border. Give it full sun and
a well drained situation and it will
reward you with at least a month of
fragrant bloom.

E. kotschyanum. This is a neat little ground cover or rock garden plant
with tiny, bright yellow flowers in
spring and dense, medium green
foliage, only 3 in. tall. It is a quick
spreader, adapting itself around rocks
in a charming way, attractive even
when out of bloom.

E. linifolium 'Variegatum'. A
rather awkward-looking plant when
young, it soon settles itself in a comfort-
able position in the garden and grows
into a low, wide mound, about 18 in.
tall. The leaves are grayish-green with
cream-colored margins and clothe the
stems to the base. The flowers undergo
a curious color change, beginning rosy-
orange and gradually becoming a soft
purple as they age. The main flush of

Erysimum 'Bowles Mauve'

bloom is in the spring, but scattered flowers are produced throughout the summer. The variegated foliage makes the plant attractive all year round. It does not seem to produce seeds, but is readily propagated by cuttings.

E. pulchellum. This species grows in low clumps, sometimes many-headed. The spatulate leaves are green and the flowers a rich shade of orange like California poppies, blooming in the spring. It is easy to grow and seeds itself about the garden, though it is never a nuisance.

E. concinnum. (*E. suffrutescens*). BEACH WALLFLOWER, POINT REYES WALLFLOWER. This Pacific Coast native actually inhabits the cliffs above the beach, rather than the beach itself. It is a much-branched, shrubby little plant, about 18 in. tall, and somewhat succulent. The leaves are narrow and gray-green, the flowers pale yellow or cream-colored, fragrant, blooming late winter to spring. It tends to be short-lived in cultivation, so it is well to gather a few seeds as insurance, in case it does not survive the winter. Deadhead for additional bloom.

E. suffruticosum. Beginning in spring, this is a long bloomer with golden yellow flowers in compact racemes that elongate in fruit. In habit it is woody at base, erect to 20 in. and much branched. It is a prolific seeder.

E.C.G.

EUPHORBIA. *Euphorbiaceae*. SPURGE. Euphorbias, comprising a genus in the spurge family, include plants as dissimilar as the familiar poinsettia and the strange, cactus-like globes of *E. valida*. Between these extremes are some common garden weeds and some important and useful garden perennials. Most are hardy and undemanding, often more available from friends than from nurseries. Their flowers are little knobbly things set in collar-like colorful bracts at the apex of leafy stems. The leaves typically crowd together just below the inflorescence. These flowering stems are long lasting in arrangements and even more long lasting left in the garden. The cut stems, however, bleed a milky sap that, to some people, is as irritating as poison oak, so it is wise to avoid touching it or getting it in the eyes.

E. amygdaloides. This is the so-called wood spurge of Great Britain, also a wilding of Europe and Southern Asia. As the common name suggests, it is happy in some shade. Dry shade will suit it perfectly well. It forms a plant about 12 by 12 in. The stems and young foliage are mahogany-colored, and its mature leaves, rather long and narrow, are deep green with a prominent white central vein. Its yellowish blossoms are held airily in loose sprays above the branches. Not large, they seem made of gold and mahogany embroidery knots set in little collars under an inch across. Bloom is in spring and summer. Use it as a ground cover under pomegranates or to skirt a bed of *Kniphofia* or *Alstroemeria* in orange and yellow shades.

E. characias. This Mediterranean species is one of the most handsome and easiest of the euphorbias to grow. A small plant will quickly make a massive clump (5 by 4 ft.) of tall columns, fat with bluish-gray leaves and topped by chocolate-centered, brilliant chartreuse flowers in domed clusters, equally fat. They bloom in spring, remain colorful and fresh for months on the plant and last for several weeks when cut for the house. Spent stalks should be cut all the way to the ground. New stems will rise with the first autumn rains. Small, self-sown volunteers can be dug and moved, although mature plants resent root disturbance. Grow them in sun or light shade in almost any soil and be as stingy as you wish with summer water. Their great size and sharp color make them difficult bedfellows in mixed borders or small gardens. They are unabashed show-offs, so give them room of their own. Use them in masses to brighten a background of ivy or dark shrubbery, or, if you fancy a tropical look, try them with big, glossy fatsias. *E. wulfenii* is sometimes considered a sub-species rather than a separate species; its most conspicuous difference is that its bracts are more yellow than greenish and lack the dark centers of *E. characias*.

E. epithymoides. An east European native that wants sunshine, well-drained soil, and moderate to little water, this is a useful plant for droughty sections of the garden. In humid weather, however, it may wilt and decline. It was once called *E. polychroma*, perhaps because of its multi-hued coloration when in flower, which is in early spring. The bracts are set densely in 3 in. heads, bright golden at the top and a greener yellow below, gradually blending into narrow, light green leaves. The plant makes bushy, 18 by 18 in. hummocks if kept cut, leggier if left to its own devices, and disappears in winter. It is valuable for flower arrangements. Grow it with purple-flowered plants like irises, *Campanula glomerata* or heliotrope.

E. myrsinites. From southern Europe this low-growing spurge has foot-long trailing stems thickly clad with smooth, gray-green, over-lapping leaves with pointed tips which bear the flowers in late winter. It is grown for its unusual form, however, rather than for its blossoms. These are yellow-green stars in little collars that become pinkish with age. It needs excellent drainage to be grown at the edge of a border, but to make the most of its striking design, it should rest on a sloping bank or atop a dry wall. It belongs with plants that tolerate dryish sites, with snow-in-summer (*Cerastium tomentosum*), sedums, or our western buckwheats, the eriogonums. Specimens can be found in specialty nurseries, but most often it is grown from seed.

E. robbiae. A native of Asia Minor, this plant can put up with poor, rooty soil in dry shade. In better conditions it may spread rapidly underground. In late spring it produces lime-green, flat,

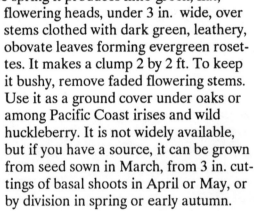

flowering heads, under 3 in. wide, over stems clothed with dark green, leathery, obovate leaves forming evergreen rosettes. It makes a clump 2 by 2 ft. To keep it bushy, remove faded flowering stems. Use it as a ground cover under oaks or among Pacific Coast irises and wild huckleberry. It is not widely available, but if you have a source, it can be grown from seed sown in March, from 3 in. cuttings of basal shoots in April or May, or by division in spring or early autumn.

E. seguierana niciciana. Originally from Turkey, this spurge is just getting known here. One of its most endearing qualities is an ability to keep its lime-yellow bloom fresh-looking all summer, even if the weather is hot and dry. Numerous stems with blue-gray leaves are topped with dainty flowers. It is a clumping plant, about 18 by 18 in., not running like some of its relatives. The cultural requirements are good drainage, average water, and plenty of sun. Try it with gray-leaved plants, large border sedums, or agapanthus.

A.R.
M.V.

Euphorbia seguieriana niciciana

FRANCOA ramosa. *Saxifragaceae*. MAIDEN'S WREATH. This native of Chile must be about the easiest plant to grow in our climate. All it needs is a little shade. Full sun will burn the foliage and wilt the flower stalks. It isn't fussy about soil, although, like most shade dwellers, it will grow more luxuriantly in humusy soil than in stiff clay. It doesn't demand fertilizer, and garden pests seem to leave it alone. The leaves grow from a basal clump that forms shoots at the sides as the plant matures. The clumps stand a foot or two high and become equally wide. The leaves, 6 to 8 in. long, are a little rough with wavy margins and deep-set veins and resemble a larger, coarser version of a dandelion leaf. The flowers appear in early summer. They are tiny blossoms along the upper foot or so of long, 2 to 3 ft. tall stalks. The color most often grown is white, but there is a very beautiful pink. Both the foliage and the flowers are treasures to flower arrangers. The plants grow vigorously all year round, getting quite crowded, so it is best to start new plants from offshoots every few years. Plants can be found in nurseries, but cuttings can usually be had from friends when they are tidying up their overgrown specimens. If you ask your friend how to root the cuttings, you will probably be told, "Just stick 'em in the ground and and they'll grow." And they will. To show off the flowers on their wandlike stems, plant them against a background of shrubbery with dark green foliage. They look well among patches of ferns. At the front of the bed you might enjoy a low-growing edger such as one of the campanulas.

M.V.

GERANIUM. *Geraniaceae*. CRANESBILL. While there are over 300 species, the family contains only a few genera. One of them, *Pelargonium*, which will not be treated here, has been given, confusedly, the common name, "geranium", while the genus described here is sometimes called "true geranium". However, we will not worry ourselves about common names; these are botanically geraniums and all are perennial.

The species are semi-evergreen, but they should be trimmed back, part or all the way to the ground, in late fall or earliest spring for renewal of the foliage. Mostly they form low, leafy mounds of palmately divided leaves. Many species have stems that spread or trail, some as long as 2 ft. All species are good on a slope or in containers. They are attractive as an edging or mixed with other perennials. Flowering is from spring through fall and will be more profuse in the sun, though there will be some bloom even in the shade. The flowers come in white, pink, lavender, magenta, and blue, often with a contrasting veining. They require ordinary garden soil and constant moisture. Here are a few kinds that have been tested in the gardens of the Peninsula.

G. cinereum 'Ballerina'. A charming, low-growing plant that gradually builds into a mass about 1-1/2 ft. in diameter. The rounded leaves are gray-green and die to the ground in winter. Lilac-pink flowers with dark veins and very dark centers appear mid-summer and continue blooming for about a month. They are in harmony with the size and color of the leaves. 'Ballerina' would make a fine edging for a herbaceous border or a rock garden. Some protection given by taller plants is desirable in full sun. Good drainage and friable soil are also necessary in order to build up a good plant.

G. dalmaticum. The leaves are quite small, the low clumps tight and slow to form. The flowers are pale pink or white.

G. incanum. A prolific self seeder! Invasive? Easy to pull out. It makes a dense mound, but will trail on a slope. If you live in a frost pocket, you may find this too tender, though it will recover from a light frost. It produces numerous, bright magenta flowers from spring to fall.

G. 'Johnson's Blue'. Different writers place this hybrid differently, but there is only one 'Johnson's Blue'. It is a good violet-blue with a white eye; it grows about 18 in. tall and disappears in winter.

G. macrorrhizum 'Album'.
Selected by Walter Ingwersen,
this is a charming plant for shady
spots in the border or rock garden. It makes a mound about 8 to
10 in. high and over 1 ft. across.
Some gardeners use 'Album' as a
ground cover because its soft,
hairy leaves persist through the
winter. The hairs carry glands
that release a very pleasing
fragrance. In Europe it has long
been used medicinally and in perfume. Early summer brings the
heaviest flowering, but there will
be occasional blossoms year-
round. The flowers are nicely
scented with creamy-white petals,
pink calyces, and long pink
stamens. 'Album' requires a minimum of water, but needs to be
situated in soil that contains lots
of humus. Propagation is by
division of the rhizomes from the
mother clump. 'Bevan's Variety'
is a selection that is similar to
'Alba' in habit and culture, but
has vivid magenta flowers.

G. × magnificum. Coming
into bloom in early summer, this
spreading plant is truly magnificent. Mid-green, hairy leaves
rise about 1 ft. from the ground
and continue to look acceptably
good throughout the winter.
Flowers are a rich purplish-violet,
the size of a fifty cent piece, and
stand well above the foliage. Half-
day direct sun and strong light apparently stimulate flowering. A
friable soil and moderate watering are necessities. In my garden,

Geranium macrorrhizum 'Album'

this sterile hybrid repeats bloom sporadically and has more or less evergreen foliage. The contrary to both items is reported by English gardeners.

G. palmatum. Be sure to give this short-lived perennial lots of space, for it will develop deeply-divided leaves over 1 ft. wide and leaf stalks 3 ft. high. In midsummer this giant breaks into bloom with deep pink flowers, a delightful sight in a shady border. By late summer the hairs on the tall stalks are quite fuzzy and the color of the stalks turns pale magenta. Only mature plants have this surprising feature. Fertile seeds are abundant, and due to a carpel ejection device, plantlets are to be found quite a distance from the mother plant. Cultural conditions include shade, soil with lots of humus, and regular waterings.

E.B.
B.C.

GYPSOPHILA paniculata. *Caryophyllaceae*. BABY'S BREATH. The classic florists' bouquet filler is also interesting for its cloud effect in borders. To 3 ft. tall and wide, this profusely branched, almost woody-based perennial is a profusion of thousands of tiny 1/4 in. white flowers on diffusely panicled pedicels. Leaves to 3 in. long become almost unnoticeable.

All varieties need a sunny, well-drained, neutral to alkaline soil, which need not be rich. Cut plants back to 6 to 8 in. from the ground in fall. Propagation is easy from seed in spring or in the case of named forms, from cuttings in late spring. Do not try to move an established plant; it has a tap root. Baby's breath is great, of course, as a cut flower and also in dried arrangements.

Available varieties include: 'Bristol Fairy', taller, to 4 ft. with dense, double, white flowers; 'Flore Pleno', 3 ft. tall with double flowers; 'Rosy Veil', dwarf 1-1/2 ft. with white to pink double flowers.

B.Y.

HEDYCHIUM gardneranum. *Zingiberaceae*. KAHILI GINGER. Growing to 8 ft. tall, this semi-tropical ginger from India does well at the back of a bed against a south-facing wall under the eaves. The eaves will give protection from frost and the wall the required heat for good flower production. Given these conditions, this ginger should do well any place on the Peninsula.

Each rhizome sends up a single stalk, not unlike a broad-leaved corn stalk, making a striking pattern against a wall, and producing a large, handsome cluster of extremely fragrant flowers at the tip. They are a deep yellow with bright red stamens, and even one of the small flowers can scent a room.

I cut off the old stalks each winter and get better flowering from the new ones that reliably shoot up in the spring. After three or four years the plants will need to be dug, the old, non-productive part of the rhizome removed, and the plant re-positioned, much as with iris. Fertilize in the spring and give regular water.

K.B.

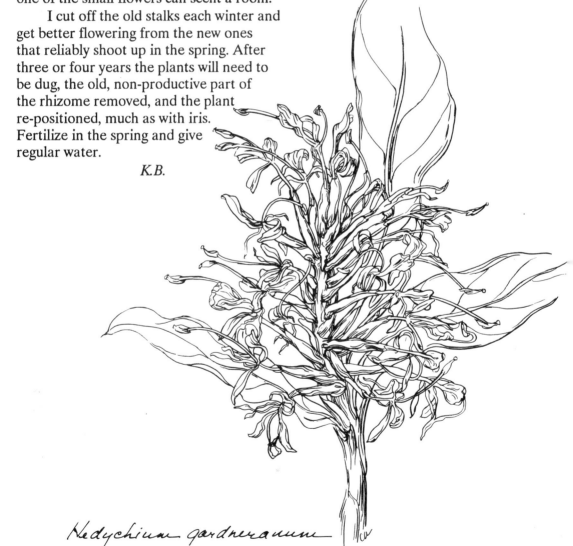

Hedychium gardneranum

HELIANTHEMUM nummularium. *Cistaceae.* SUN ROSE. Helianthemums fall into that gray area between shrubs and perennials that, for want of a better term, we call subshrubs. They are sturdy, evergreen, sun-loving, and drought tolerant. Usually under 12 in. high, they will spread into a dense 3 ft. mat. They look and bloom best where they have very good drainage and some summer water and are especially suitable for banks, rock gardens, and as edgers.

H. nummularium is the name under which most helianthemums are sold in nurseries, although they are probably hybrids with other species. The foliage may be green or gray, the small, simple leaves entirely covering the twiggy plants. The five-petalled flowers with their central tuft of stamens do bear some resemblance to tiny, single roses, hence the common name. Flowers are small, about 1 in. across, but numerous, and produced in abundance over several weeks in the spring, with scattered blooms into the summer. A wide range of color is available, and some varieties have double flowers. The gray-leaved forms may have pink or yellow flowers, the green-leaved forms, white, yellow, apricot, orange, and red. As with many shrubby perennials, helianthemums tend to become leggy and woody at the base unless they are sheared back after flowering. Propagation by cuttings is not difficult and it is always easy to find a spot in the garden for these adaptable plants.

E.C.G.

HELIANTHUS angustifolius. (*H. salicifolius, H. orgyalis*). *Asteraceae. (Compositae)*. The SWAMP SUNFLOWER is native to the marshlands of the middle and southern Atlantic states, and as the common name suggests, it wants both sun and water. It is completely herbaceous, and is slow to achieve its ultimate height of 6 to 7 ft. The leaves are long and narrow, as the species name indicates. The stalks grow in clumps and branch at the top to hold many bright yellow, daisy-like flowers with purple centers. The brilliance of the yellow and the height of the display make the plant difficult to use in the garden, but since the bloom is in the fall, the color will be welcome. You might plant a clump behind the lower-growing, white or lavender *Physostegia virginiana*. There will be some overlapping in their time of bloom. Or try *Echinops exaltatus*, another late

bloomer. A different way to grow
the plant is to peg down the tips of
the tallest growth, which will encourage bud break along the stalks
for a long shower of bloom.
Propagation is by division in the
spring. Ordinary garden soil is fine.
K.B.

HELICHRYSUM. *Asteraceae. (Compositae)*.

H. angustifolium. CURRY PLANT.
Native to the Mediterranean, this
is a rather upright to spreading
shrubby plant with narrow, almost
white leaves. The common name
results from the fragrance of this
plant when crushed, but it is not
used in cooking. A rather quick
grower, it should be trimmed back
often to be kept looking tidy. The
bloom is a dusty yellow in spring.
'Nana' is a miniature form well
suited to the rock garden or to give
a spot of gray at the edge of the
border. Both should be drought
tolerant.

Helianthus angustifolius

H. petiolatum. (*H. petiolare*).
Native to South Africa, this sub-
shrub can become a broad 6 to 8 ft. mass if it has something on
which to scramble. Grown for the gray to almost white roundish
leaves and stems, this plant makes a drought tolerant ground or
bank cover in full sun. The small flowers form at the end of the
branches, but should be sheared off to prevent production of the
rather irritating fluff of the dead flowers. It may be necessary to
shear more than once a year to keep it from looking shaggy.
'Limelight' is a form with lemon yellow foliage that is a much more
restrained plant than the gray form. It can be quite effective at
twilight or with night lighting. It will do best in just a little shade so

the leaves won't burn. 'Variegatum' has gray leaves with yellow markings.

H. psilolepis 'Moe's Gold'. This makes a flat mat covered with small silvery leaves and yellow everlasting flowers in the summer and fall. A rapid grower when first planted, it may need some pinching to form a tight mat.

E.C.

HELIOTROPIUM arborescens. *Boraginaceae.* HELIOTROPE comes from Peru, as its old name of *H. peruvianum* suggests. Like many plants from that region of the world, it is somewhat tender to frost. Although the plant size is variable up to 4 ft. tall, it can easily be kept to 2 ft. The leaves are 2 in. long, heavily veined, dark green, and soft to the touch. The flowers, white to purple, are individually very small but form tight clusters about 1 to 1-1/2 in. across. Partial shade, average moisture, and soil with some humus are the requirements for best growth. Bloom is in summer.

Two terms come to mind when heliotrope is mentioned: "old-fashioned" and "fragrant". This plant is an old favorite and mixes nicely with other old-fashioned plants such as lilacs, pelargoniums, iris, lilies, narcissus, and primulas. The fragrance is special, though difficult to describe. A nice foil for the dark color of this plant would be *Cerastium tomentosum* or *Oxalis crassipes*. The growth habit is loose and the stems are weak, giving it a casual look. Regular pruning will help to keep it compact. Heliotrope would be effective at the top of a wall, or in a hanging basket so that the sweet fragrance could be enjoyed at close hand. The flowers do not hold up well when cut. It can be propagated from seed or cuttings.

M.K.

HELLEBORUS. *Ranunculaceae.* Hellebores are among those plants whose virtues become more apparent the longer one lives with them. They are certainly not showy; "subdued" describes them more accurately. Because they bloom in late winter when little else is in flower, flourish in shade, are impervious to deer and gophers, and tolerate a wide range of soils and harsh conditions, they have endeared themselves to gardeners for hundreds of years. Hellebores are remarkably hardy, tolerant of many different soils and conditions. They actually prefer the alkaline soils that are common in the West, so they are one shade-loving plant that does not need acid soil. They will survive long periods of dryness and neglect, but respond enthusiastically to fertilizer and water. The best time to fertilize is just after the old, faded flowers and last year's leaf stalks have been trimmed away, then the new flush of foliage will come up with vigor. The plant is poisonous in all its parts, which is why deer and gophers generally ignore it, but snails and slugs are, unfortunately, immune, and consume it readily. Seemingly these are its only pests. Nurseries of the ordinary kind usually do not stock hellebores, but they may be obtained in some hardy plant or specialty nurseries. Any gardener who has them will have lots of seedlings to give away. There are several species of hellebores, most from Europe and the eastern Mediterranean region, but only four are usually available to the ordinary gardener.

H. argutifolius. (*H. lividus ssp. corsicus*). The CORSICAN HELLEBORE is the largest of the four, making a 2 to 3 ft. clump. The gray-green, prickly-edged foliage is considered by many to be the handsomest of all. The flowers are pale green, cup-shaped, 15 to 30 in a cluster, and the longest lasting in the garden, still looking well after the seeds have scattered. This is the most sun tolerant of the hellebores.

H. foetidus. You will have no difficulty growing this obliging species. It will grow and thrive in rooty shade and make a handsome underplanting of deep green. Mature clumps will attain a height and spread of 1-1/2 to 2 ft. The leaves are the typical, palmately divided form, but with 5 to 11 narrow-toothed leaflets. Against this very dark background the clusters of pale greenish-white, cup-shaped flowers contrast strikingly. The specific name refers to the unpleasant smell of the foliage when it is cut or bruised, but the odor is not persistent, in fact, flower arrangers are particularly fond of the leaves for their unique, blackish-green color.

H. niger. CHRISTMAS ROSE is the species most often mentioned in gardening books, but is not easily available in this country, or easily established once obtained. It comes from the mountains and meadows of the European Alps east of Yugoslavia and perhaps it resents our warm winters and dry conditions. It does best in a heavy fertile soil with ample moisture. A single, pure white flower is borne on each stalk above dark green, leathery leaves, similar to those of *H. orientalis* but with glaucous leaves that have only a few teeth

Helleborus orientalis

toward the ends of the leaflets. Several improved cultivars, notably 'Potter's Wheel', have been selected and propagated in England.

H. orientalis. LENTEN ROSE is from Turkey and the Caucasus. The time of bloom depends on climate, and in our area of mild winters the Lenten rose is usually starting into bloom by Christmas. A great deal of variation in color and form of the flowers is inherent in *H. orientalis*. The flowers, in which it is the sepals that are colored (the petals being reduced to nectaries) may be white through pink to deep purple, often speckled or splotched with a deeper color. The sepals may be rounded, pointed, or even wavy at the edges, and some hold their flowers erect, though most are pendulous. As the flower ages, the petals fall, the sepals become duller in color, and the five seed capsules inflate, filling the center of the flower. Because they cross freely and produce lots of seed that germinates easily, each spring brings out some new surprises, though even a well-grown plant takes two years to bloom. The foliage is evergreen, the leaves palmately dissected into 5 to 7 broad sharply-toothed lobes. In this species the flower and leaf stalks arise directly from the rootstock. After the seeds have ripened and been shed, the old leaf and flowering stalks can be removed, because a new flush of leaves is being produced. Each year the clump enlarges, so an especially good form or color can be increased by division.

E.C.G.

HEMEROCALLIS. *Liliaceae.* DAYLILY. Native to temperate Asia, Japan, and Europe, daylilies are closely related to hostas. Twenty-one species of hemerocallis exist, but mostly hybrids are grown today. Daylilies are fibrous-rooted, hardy perennials, usually with tuberous storage roots.

In our area they can be evergreen, deciduous, or somewhere in between. Above ground they form clumps of medium green, arching, sword-shaped leaves. The flowers are borne above the foliage on leafless stalks (scapes) that may be branched. Clusters of buds appear at the ends, opening successively into lily-like flowers, each lasting one day. Size of clumps, and proportionately the flowers, varies from miniature (3 in. flowers, maximum height of scapes 18 in.) to medium (3 to 4-1/2 in. flowers, scapes 18 to 35 in.) to tall (4-1/2 to 9 in. flowers and scapes over 36 in.).

The flower appears to be formed of six petals, but only the inner three are true petals, the outer ones are sepals. There are several types of color patterns, all of which have names. Colors range through many shades of yellow, orange, red, pink, purple, and near white. Several forms of flowers have also been defined. So you see the "common daylily" need not be a boring clump of orange or yellow flowers. There are myriads of choices, so be adventuresome!

Time of bloom is difficult to pin down, especially in our area. Daylily catalogs give guides, and with some experimentation, it's possible to have daylilies blooming or showing some semblance of bloom all year long, especially when you include the evergreen, repeat-bloom varieties. Those varieties that bloom only once during the season usually continue for at least a month.

The culture of daylilies is easy, one reason for their growing popularity. They prefer well-drained soil, but they perform well for me in my Palo Alto clay. Of course, if I were growing blooms for show, I would work much harder on the soil, but they seem to adapt to most reasonable soil conditions. They prefer sun, but will do well in part shade. They are the perfect plant for that part of the garden that gets shade in the morning and blasting sun in the afternoon. They don't require much fertilizer, perhaps a little nitrogen in the spring. It is important not to over-fertilize because this encourages gross foliage at the expense of bloom. At planting time it is recommended to mix the native soil with some well-rotted manure/compost and perhaps a handful of bone meal. Pests are not a big problem. Snails may chomp on the new growth in early spring, but once the leaves are hardened off, they don't bother to chomp any more. Divide the clumps only when their centers become obviously crowded and somewhat elevated and the production of blooms begins to diminish. With a good mulch, daylilies can go at least a week before needing water, assuming that when they are watered, they are given a "good drink". They are often recommended as one of the perennials for water conserving landscapes.

Scapes should be cut from the base when blooming is finished to prevent energy going into seed production and, over the course of the blooming season, spent foliage should be pulled from the base of the plant to keep the clumps looking well. This is more necessary for the evergreen varieties and some of the semi-evergreen varieties. The dormant varieties just die back in the fall and their foliage is easily removed at that time.

Daylilies are best planted from divisions in the early spring or fall. Those grown in gallon cans may be planted any time of year. Seed may be used as well, if you are patient, but this is not the typical means of propagation. Divisions from a friend are likely to be larger than those you receive from catalogs and can be treated like gallon can plants. In our heavy clay soils, it is best to plant them "high" so that water will run away from the crown.

In the landscape daylilies can be used in a variety of situations because of their broad tolerance of growing conditions. They have a relatively bold foliage, so they should be considered as an ingredient in the whole landscape plan and not stuck here and there in a hodge-podge fashion. They can, however, be used anywhere in the garden. One is limited only by one's imagination. A massed planting can be very dramatic, but care should be given to color selection. In front of a well-chosen mass of daylilies add a border of the annual ageratum, clumps of blue agapanthus, or *Felicia amelloides*, and you will have a real show-stopper. Daylily plants that go dormant may be under-planted with spring bulbs. As the bulb foliage dies back, it is concealed by the emerging daylily foliage.

To use daylilies as cut flowers, pick a scape that has many buds left to come. The flowers will open successively, each lasting only for a day and diminishing in size. Remove the spent flowers so as not to detract from the opening blossoms. I prefer to enjoy them on the plant, but when the daylilies are at their height, a big, informal bunch of mixed colors cut at different lengths and plopped into a glass pitcher can be breathtaking.

I order daylilies only from suppliers on the West Coast, because their growing conditions more nearly replicate mine. I have concentrated on those that repeat bloom and on the smaller varieties, because I feel their scale fits better in our smaller California gardens. I've also started to pay attention to the name of the hybridizer, which is usually listed in parentheses or italics in the catalog. For California I like those hybridized by Munson, Romine, Durio, Jablonski, and Winneford. I am sure there are many others; I just have not tried them.

Sadly, fragrance in hybrids is almost non-existent, at least to my nose. The old-fashioned, lemon yellow species, *H. lilioasphodelus*, has a delicious scent, and the hybrids that are listed as fragrant tend to be in the yellow shades. But at best, it is my experience that fragrance is dependent upon a lot of imagination and a hint of smell. Bottom line: you don't grow daylilies for fragrance — mix them with roses for fragrance.

Catalogs offer a wide variety of types, sizes, and colors, but color is truly in the eye of the beholder. Some of the lavenders I've grown looked dull and muddy to me. I've removed them from my border. The following varieties are in the salmon, tangerine, and yellow range.

Miniatures that I've grown: 'Stella De Oro' (with more water and a bit of fertilizer will bloom almost all summer), 'Bitsy', 'Bertie Ferris', 'Terra Cotta Baby', and 'Tiny Pumpkin'.

Large flowered varieties: 'Hyperion', 'Pojo', 'Tangerine', 'Prester John', 'Memorable Masterpiece', 'Sacred Shield', 'Abbeville Sunset', 'Family Party', 'Samurai Silk', 'Diamond Head', and many others to which I've sadly lost the labels. If you do not find the above varieties listed in your catalog (and they do go in and out of fashion) try some others!

P.S.

HEUCHERA. *Saxifragaceae*. ALUMROOT, CORAL BELLS. The genus *Heuchera* is entirely of North American origin with about 50 species occurring in the wild from Alaska to Mexico, although some of the most colorful named varieties have been developed by British hybridizers. Oddly, however, the genus is named for an 18th century German botanist, von Heucher. Many heucheras are well suited to garden culture, and all of them perform best in light shade in soil enriched with humus. They will quickly make large clumps of roundish or heart-shaped leaves with lobed or scalloped edges. High above these basal leaves, panicles of airy little bell-like flowers blossom on long stalks. Flower arrangers like them for the delicacy they add to flower arrangements and cutting encourages the formation of new stems, prolonging the blooming period. Even out of bloom, the plants are handsome all year round. Planting or division is best done in early autumn. To keep them looking at their best, they usually need dividing every two or three years because long, thick root stalks develop below the leaves.

H. americana. ROCK GERANIUM, AMERICAN ALUMROOT. This species grows in the wild through the center of the continent from central Canada to Louisiana in what is described as "dry woods", (surely not as dry as California woods, for here they do need some summer water). The plant grows to 3 ft. tall and has five-lobed leaves with toothed edges. In late summer greenish flowers appear formed in panicles, each little blossom urn-shaped with conspicuously protruding stamens. This species is not grown for its flowers, however, but rather for the color and texture of its leaves.

H. maxima. ISLAND ALUMROOT. This species originated in the Channel Islands off the Santa Barbara coast, but thrives in California gardens. During the summer when it blooms, it is readily available in many garden centers. The plants grow to 2 ft. tall with lobed and toothed leaves, four inches or more long, and a little fluted rather than flat on stalks about 8 in. long. The leaf color is a bright, light green, the texture smooth above and roughly hairy beneath. Smaller leaves clasp the lower portion of the elegant flower stems which bear long clusters of small white blossoms. This plant can tolerate morning sun and is somewhat drought tolerant. In the Santa Barbara Botanic Garden it grows in a large, dramatic bed under a spreading oak, but in our smaller home gardens, it is useful under large Japanese maples and dogwoods, or in front of *Pieris* where it combines well with western irises and hellebores.

H. 'Palace Purple'. In this cultivar, sometimes listed as a cultivar of *H. americana* or *H. micrantha*, the leaves are a satiny, dark, almost olive green on top, but on the reverse are plum-colored and roughly hairy, matching the petiole and the flower stalk. The leaves will seem almost invisible among other dark-foliaged plants, but at the edge of a brick patio and with light green maidenhair ferns behind them, they will command attention. Not every garden center carries this plant, but it can be obtained from nurseries that specialize in unusual perennials.

H. sanguinea. CORAL BELLS may be best known as border plants along paths, but they make a more substantial spring display in big patches among sword ferns and wood ferns and with campanulas or glossy bergenias. The most substantial display, however, will be made by the Bressingham hybrids developed in England, the coral bells most growers have offered in recent years. The plants are larger with taller flower stalks and a greater range of flower color than the southwestern species. Reds are redder and pinks pinker, some even salmon-colored, while others are bicolored with white rims. The leaves are dull green, rough-textured, shallowly lobed, the edges scalloped rather than toothed, the leaf stalks softly hairy.

M.V.

x **HEUCHERELLA** '**Bridget Bloom**'. *Saxifragaceae.* A hybrid between two North American genera, *Heuchera* and *Tiarella*, this plant was named by its British developer, Alan Bloom, for his wife. It is a cheerful plant with clumps of bright, ground-hugging leaves and flower spikes growing to 1 ft. tall, spangled with blossoms of the clearest pink, much like coral bells, but more thickly set. The leaves are yellowy-green with pinkish veins and long brownish stalks, just a little roughly hairy. They need a bit of shade and some summer water. Columbines and campanulas are good companions for them in the garden, but if you are lucky enough to have a stand of lily-of-the-valley, that would be even better. And, of course, ferns are a wonderful foil. You will find *Heucherella* for sale in garden centers during the last cool, rainy months as their buds begin to form. Get them into the ground quickly so that you can enjoy their rapid growth and heavy blossoming.

M.V.

HUNNEMANIA fumariifolia. *Papaveraceae.* MEXICAN TULIP POPPY. This plant, unlike many that are named for their discoverers, is named for a 19th century English seed agent, John Hunneman, who sold seeds others collected. Originally from the high country of Mexico, the tulip poppy needs a warm spot in full sun with excellent drainage. Once established, it requires little water, but in shade or with excessive water or damp, it will quickly rot away. Some gardeners prefer to treat it as an annual, but in a spot to their liking, plants can go on for years. Grown in front of the taller, electric blue blossoms of *Anchusa azurea* 'Dropmore' or 'Loddon Royalist', their brilliant yellow flowers are particularly dazzling. They bloom through summer and fall. The plants are bushy, with erect stems to 3 ft. tall. The leaves are smooth, blue-gray, up to 4 in. long, and finely dissected, looking much like the California poppy to which *Hunnemania* is closely related. Unlike the California poppy, however, whose flower buds are enclosed in a single cap resembling a long, pointed dunce cap, the buds of tulip poppy are rounded and enclosed in a two-parted, pale green calyx much like Iceland poppy buds. The flowers, rich yellow with many orange stamens in the center, are cupped, about three inches across, with four petals that are slightly ruffled at the rim. The blossoms are solitary on long stalks and, unlike most poppies, hold up well for cutting. The seed capsule is a 3 in. needlelike tube much like that of the California poppy. As it develops, it spears through the center of the flower days before the petals fall. The capsule contains many tiny seeds. They are slow to germinate and usually do not self-sow in the garden. To propagate them, sow the seeds in a sandy medium during autumn or early spring indoors or in a greenhouse that is kept dryish, not humid. Disturb the roots as little as possible when moving them into pots or setting them out in the garden. It is easier, of course, just to buy plants already started, and although they are less readily available than petunias and marigolds, they can be found; ask your favorite nursery to order them for you.

M.V.

Nunnemannia fumarifolia

I

IBERIS. *Brassicaceae. (Cruciferae)*. CANDYTUFT. Both of the perennial species given here are good edging plants and are somewhat similar in appearance. Both have narrow, dark, evergreen leaves, growing up stems, woody at the base, to 12 in. or more and both form small, dense clumps. They thrive in sun or part shade and bloom from early spring to June, the flowers in round, flat heads. Both accept ordinary garden watering and soil and are somewhat drought tolerant.

I. gibraltarica. This is the more colorful species. The flowers on mine open white and soon turn lilac. So far my plants have not formed as dense clumps as *I. sempervirens*, but they self-sow and the

Iberis sempervirens

seedlings are agreeable to transplanting. I also find that this species does better in more shade. Certainly the plants look better and the bloom lasts longer.

I. sempervirens. Often used for a border along a walk or even as a small hedge around an island bed, this species has several cultivars growing to different heights. 'Little Gem' is the shortest, 4 to 6 in. ; 'Snowflake' extends to 12 in. in height and spreads easily to 24 in. across, but can be sheared for a more formal appearance. The white flowers are in flat clusters and should be sheared just after bloom for a sprinkling of re-bloom later.

K.B.

INCARVILLEA arguta. *Bignoniaceae.* The incarvilleas are fleshy-rooted perennials from Asia. This one is smaller in all details than the better known *I. delavayi.* The pinnate leaves arise from the base as well as along the reddish stems and have a touch of bronze that keeps them from being too showy in the landscape. The flowers are pink, tubular blossoms about 1 in. in length and are borne in racemes. The plant grows some 18 in. tall with a wider spread. Its habit makes it a good candidate for a walltop where its weak stems can spill over and present its terminal flowers for observation. Flowering is in early summer.

My own plant has lived through one winter in fine condition. It did not go dormant as *I. delavayi* seems to. During the summer, it received average garden water and plenty of sun. Try combining this plant with *Spiraea* 'Anthony Waterer' and species geraniums.

M.K.

KNIFOPHIA uvaria. *Liliaceae*. POKER PLANT. The "Red Hot Poker" of old gardens is still a useful, if common, plant for gardens today. There are also some newer varieties with different habits and flower color. In general the plants grow in a clump of long, to 3 ft., grass-like foliage from which taller stalks rise with spikes of red, orange, and yellow tubular flowers. I have two varieties. The common one keeps its foliage through the year and seems to require little water. The cultivar, possibly 'White Fairy', has a cream-colored blossom that appears in early summer. If the plant gets dry, the flower stalks will flop over and only the tips will rise again. It goes dormant in the fall, necessitating removal of the old foliage. In both plants some grooming is required through the year. The flowers pass, leaving bare stalks, and the foliage can get shabby. In spite of all this, the plants are well worth growing. The flowers are a delight to hummingbirds for their nectar and to flower arrangers for their strong vertical line and long-lasting quality. Propagation is by division.

K.B.

LAMIUM maculatum. *Lamiaceae. (Labiatae).* DEAD NETTLE. This decumbent, trailing, evergreen perennial is used in hanging baskets and as a ground cover under shade. With rich soil and abundant moisture it is an aggressive colonizer, rooting along its stems, but in a dry situation under trees, it can be attractive and controllable. The plain green form is un-distinguished, but *L. maculatum* 'Variegatum' has heart-shaped, toothed leaves with an irregular streak of white along the midrib, giving a peculiarly metallic look, like aluminum paint. The pinkish-mauve flowers that appear in early summer are pleasant in an understated way. The cultivar 'Beacon Silver' is more attractive and desirable and a bit less aggressive. Its leaves are white with a green edge, good for lighting up a shady corner. Another named cultivar is 'White Nancy', with leaves like 'Beacon Silver', but white flowers instead of mauve.

E.C.G.

LAVANDULA. *Lamiaceae. (Labiatae).* LAVENDER. When we lather up with Yardley's lavender scented soap, we are continuing a 2000 year tradition. Lavender gets its name from *lavo*, Latin, "to wash", because of its popularity with the ancient Romans who used it to scent their baths. With plants that have been in cultivation for such a long time, origins get blurred, but most authorities believe that English lavender, *L. angustifolia*, came from the Mediterranean region, French lavender, *L. dentata*, from Spain, Spanish lavender *L. stoechas*, the one the Romans used, from Portugal. All of which may make the point that, however confusing Latin names may seem, at times they are less so than the common names. All the lavenders have the same cultivation needs--full sun, lean diet, good drainage. They are drought resistant, have few insect pests, and are easy to propagate from cuttings.

L. angustifolia. ENGLISH LAVENDER. Although really a shrub, English lavender has made its way into the perennial border by virtue its fragrance, its symmetrical, rounded form, and its profusion of flowers. The foliage is gray, the leaves narrow, 2-1/2 in. long by less than 1/4 in. wide, with smooth, inrolled edges. The plant will get quite large, 3 ft. in height and spread, with the flower spikes rising another foot or more above the foliage. The lavender flowers are borne in a congested spike at the top of the stiff stems. This is the species most often used for sachets, but to obtain the maximum the species most often used for sachets, but to obtain the maximum fragrance, one should cut the flowers at the height of bloom and dry them in a shady, well-ventilated place. In any case, shear after bloom to keep the plant compact and symmetrical. English lavender is often used as a hedge or edging. For this purpose the plants should be set on 18 in. centers and pruned back each spring nearly to the previous season's growth to maintain the shape. There are several cultivars that are smaller than the species and easier to use in the garden for that reason. *L.a.* 'Hidcote' is about a foot high, has very gray leaves, deep purple flowers and stays quite compact. *L.a.* 'Jean Davis', one foot high and wide, has flowers that are just on the pink side of lavender. In cold weather the foliage turns an interesting slaty purple. *L.a.* 'Munstead Dwarf' can be kept very low and compact and is the lavender used in the knot garden at Filoli. It bears a profusion of bluish-purple flowers and comes in bloom earlier than the other cultivars of *L. angustifolia*. Its foliage is shorter, greener and more compact than 'Hidcote'.

L. dentata. FRENCH LAVENDER. A very different looking plant from English lavender, *L. dentata* is not quite as big or symmetrical, and the foliage is greener. The leaves are small and narrow with square-toothed edges. The flowers are in short, dense spikes at the top of foot-long, wiry stems, but the color comes mostly from the bracts, and especially the larger bracts at the top. *L. dentata* comes as close to everblooming and indestructible as plants get. It will take full sun, poor soil, very little summer water, and bloom continuously from the time it is still in the cutting flat, all summer, and even through the winter, if it is a mild one. In fact, it is hard to find a time to prune it without sacrificing a new crop of flowers. *L.d. balearica* is a gray-foliaged form of good substance but less fragrance.

L. stoechas. SPANISH LAVENDER. The smooth edges of its gray, linear leaves are like English lavender, but its flowering spike resembles French lavender in being short, almost knobby, with a tuft of large purple bracts at the very top. The plant is 2 to 3 ft. in height. Both the flowers and the foliage are very aromatic; this is one of the species used commercially for scent. Spanish lavender is the least hardy of the lavenders, although it survives our usually mild winters out-of-doors.

E.C.G.

LEONOTIS. *Lamiaceae. (Labiatae)*. LION'S EAR. The genus includes about 30 species of annual and perennial herbs and shrubs occurring in tropical Africa and one in the East Indies. The two given below favor a warm to very warm climate, loamy soil, and moderate irrigation. Both are propagated readily by cuttings, and the second by seed. The common name for the genus, lion's ear, comes from a fancied likeness of the flower to a lion's ear.

L. leonurus. LION'S TAIL. This species is perhaps best classified as a sub-shrub in this area. Orange flowers in widely spaced, dense whorls appear in spikes from mid-August through October. What a grand color to see and work with in the fall of the year! Perhaps a combination with *Phlomis fruticosa*, the yellow-flowered Jerusalem sage, would be good for the back of a border since both plants attain 3 to 4 ft. in height and 2 to 3 ft. in width. A medium-sized *Phormium* selected for dark bronze leaves or zinnias selected in golds and deep reds would enliven the fall border. Prune to the ground in early winter.

L. nepetaefolia. Though best treated in this area as an

Leonotis leonurus

annual, it is gradually becoming naturalized in the mild areas of Mexico and California. Given a long growing season, it can attain 7 ft. in height but will remain about 2 to 3 ft. in width. Pair this spectacular orange-flowered plant with the 7 ft. *Helianthus angustifolius* for a striking color combination. Bloom, similar to *L. leonurus*, lasts from late summer until frost. Save seed for the next season.

B.C.

LIGULARIA tussilaginea. *Asteraceae. (Compositae)*. Here is a tough, handsome, easy-care plant for shade. The large leaves are somewhat kidney-shaped and are borne singly on long petioles rising some 2 ft. above the ground. The flowers, simple yellow daisies which appear occasionally on tall stalks, are unimportant. The foliage patterns, however, can be quite striking. The splashiest variegation occurs in 'Argentea'. Irregular white to ivory markings set off a dark green background. The markings may be narrow or broadly pie-shaped. 'Aureo-maculata' is called LEOPARD PLANT because of its yellow spots, while 'Gold Edge' has a narrow band of yellow around the perimeter of the leaf. 'Crispata' is not variegated, but the edge of the leaf is quite attractively crinkled and frilled. The difficulty with these cultivars is that, with the exception of 'Aureo-maculata', they are difficult to find. Pete Sugawara of the old Montebello Nursery brought many from Japan, but his fine nursery now grows houses. You might put a note in the "Plants Wanted" column of *Pacific Horticulture*. Once you have a source, propagation is by division. Snail bait, regular summer water, occasional fertilizer, and a shady location will keep the plants healthy. They make excellent container specimens.

K.B.

LIMONIUM perezii. *Plumbaginaceae*. SEA LAVENDER, STATICE. Native to the Canary Islands. The flower stalks grow up to 3 ft. tall and the plants spread to about 2 ft. The flowers are in flat-topped panicles with purple calyx and tiny, white corolla. The grayish green leaves grow up to 12 in. long including stalk.

This very satisfactory plant will bloom almost all year when there is no frost. In frosty years it will usually bloom again about a month after the last frost. Plants are damaged at around 25°F., but usually survive removal of unsightly leaves. It flowers in full sun or partial shade, and when established it requires no summer water. Snails munch on the leaves, but do not damage the flower stalks.

The bright purple color, drought tolerance, and long blooming period make limonium a very useful plant for hot, dry gardens. Seedlings appear after the rains, but only in the vicinity of their parents. These new plants will survive with no summer water and after a wet winter will even flower the first year. The plants develop tap roots, so are best acquired in six packs, available at most nurseries.

Limonium combines well with non-thirsty, gray-foliaged plants such as lavenders and artemisias, pink-flowered plants such as *Lantana montevidensis*, geraniums or diascias, or white-flowered plants such as *Cistus ladanifer* or *Dietes vegeta*.

D.D.

LYCHNIS coronaria. *Carophyllaceae*. MULLEIN PINK. This easy to grow perennial is from the Mediterranean region and so is well suited to our own growing conditions. The foliage, densely white-felted in compact, foot high, basal clumps, is attractive in itself. The numerous, branched, flowering stems rise another 2 ft. above the foliage and are felt-covered like the leaves . The flowers, borne from early summer to late fall, have five, rounded, somewhat flaring petals in a flat, phlox-like head. In color, the flowers may be any shade of red, tending toward the purple end of the spectrum, with a definite leaning toward magenta, but the brilliance of the flowers is balanced by the cool, silky-white foliage. For a more restrained color scheme, however, there are named cultivars, 'Alba', pure white, and 'Oculata', white with a bright pink eye. The cultural requirements of lychnis include full sun, good drainage, and summer water, though it is not a thirsty plant. In return for these modest demands, it will give a profusion of flowers all summer long. It is easily grown from seed, and in fact, once established it self-seeds freely.

E.C.G.

MACLEAYA. *Papaveraceae.* PLUME POPPY.

M. cordata. Sometimes listed as *Bocconia cordata,* this is a bold herbaceous perennial, native to China and Japan, grown primarily for the rounded, lobed, blue-gray foliage. These should be used as specimen plants, as they may reach 7 ft. in height and can be most effective when back lighted by the sun. Bloom is in panicles of small, white flowers in summer.

M. microcarpa is a similar species, but is a more aggressive spreader and can form a sizable patch unless controlled. 'Coral Plume' has clusters of small, coral-red, fluffy flowers. Both species are very easy to grow from root cuttings.

E.C.

MIMULUS. (DIPLACUS). *Scrophulariaceae.* MONKEY FLOWER. There are many species of *Mimulus,* annual, perennial, and shrubby. Here we are describing the shrubby sort, often called *Diplacus,* and once considered a separate genus, though now lumped into mimulus – again! These are excellent plants for your perennial border. I often tell people to think of them as marguerite daisies – they are wonderful for about 3 to 5 years, then they tend to get too woody and should be replaced. They will live for a long time, as marguerites do, but most of us like having a shapely, well-blooming plant. Always, always pinch these plants back when they are very young. Yes, you will be removing some of the flowers, but you will have a much better, healthier plant. Healthier, because these plants tend to become very brittle with age and if allowed to get too leggy are much more likely to literally fall apart. These plants are fairly drought tolerant and are deer proof. As with most of our native plants, these should be planted a bit higher than the surrounding soil level so that water does not drain towards the crown (stem) of the plant; 1/4 in. higher is fine. Good drainage is a definite plus also. The plants make wonderful container specimens, especially when used with some cascading plants like sweet alyssum, lobelia, or yerba buena.

There are many fine hybrids available. The best of these are often mistaken for azaleas when they are in full bloom. If you can bring yourself to cut them back in late July or early August (they will still be blooming at this time, and I cut them back below the oldest flowers) they will re-bloom for you in September and October.

Most of these plants are sold by color only, but at Yerba Buena Nursery some have been named. A list of some of the names and colors follows.

By name:
'Chili Red' (a complex blend of red, gold, white, and yellow)

'Grape Jelly' (best in part shade)

'Brick Red'

'V-8'

'Buff Ruffles'

By color:
Large-flowered yellows

Large-flowered white (best in part shade)

Large-flowered bright, clear red

Tangerine shades

Yellow with red spangles

Pale yellow with orange lines
Pink shades (best in part shade)

Cream (best in part shade, sometimes fades to white and sometimes doesn't)
            B.O'B.

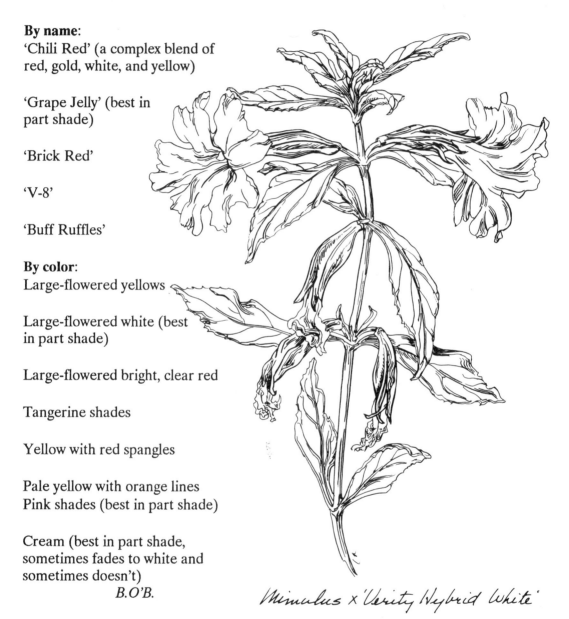

Mimulus × 'Verity Hybrid White'

NEPETA. *Lamiaceae. (Labiatae).* CATMINT. The ancient Latin name used by Pliny was probably from Nepi in Italy. Perhaps 250 species of this genus are found in temperate climates in Europe, Asia, North Africa, and mountains of tropical Africa. There are about 14 species and hybrids in cultivation. All described here require gritty soil, good drainage, and lots of sunlight. The common name "catmint" is presently used for the entire genus.

N. cataria. This is the plant long known as CATNIP and grown for its attractiveness to cats. Before tea from China was brought to England, Frances A. Bardswell informs us that catnip tea was a widely enjoyed drink, and was also used medicinally for colds, nervous headaches, and as a spring tonic. Many still grow it for its pretty blue flowers and undemanding ways. It grows 2 to 3 ft. tall and is a good plant for a rough piece of ground.

N. x faassenii. A charming plant is this sterile hybrid and one that is superior in many respects to *N. mussinii*, with which it is often confused (see below). *N. x faassenii* grows to about 24 in. and bears lovely pale lavender flowers on long spikes. The silver-gray leaves are handsome, and in this climate remain evergreen throughout the winter. In the border it is an invaluable plant for pools of lavender color which it produces, off and on, spring through fall. One needs to cut back the flowering stems after full bloom is reached--this takes courage, but the reward is another flowering. Propagation is by division or cuttings in midsummer. The front of a border could be enhanced with a drift of this nepeta, or the canes of roses such as 'General Kleger' or 'Dainty Bess' could be hidden.

N. mussinii has similar properties to catnip, but has graceful wands of lavender flowers set off with gray-green foliage. This is the plant Gertrude Jekyll said could hardly be overpraised, while William Robinson banned it from the garden! When established it will set large crops of fertile seed, proving to be a blessing if seedlings can be shared, or a nuisance if they must be weeded. By pruning to the crown while still in full bloom in early June, there will be a repeat full bloom in midsummer. In our mild climate this procedure may be repeated still a second time. In nurseries you may find this species sometimes confused with *N. x faassenii*.

N. siberica. From southern Siberia, Mongolia, and Kansu this species was introduced into cultivation about 1760. It has only recently grown into popularity. With underground runners it slowly increases, giving rise to spikes of violet-blue flowers in whorls that attain 2 ft. in height. Smooth leaves of fresh green are spaced well apart on the stem. Blooming takes place for about one month beginning in late May or early June, depending on the weather. It is quite lovely with the pink-flowered *Erodium chamaedryoides roseum* or *Geranium endressi* 'Wargrave Pink'. All these plants take a moderately heavy soil, full to almost full sunlight, and lots of compost. For abundant foliage and flowers, feed with a balanced fertilizer several times during the growing season.

B.C.

Nepeta mussinii

O

OENOTHERA. *Onagraceae.* EVENING PRIMROSE. A genus of annual, biennial, or perennial herbs, it has 80 species occurring naturally in the new world. Though commonly known as "Evening Primrose", some species are day-flowering and are called "Suncups" or "Sundrops". Almost all have fragrance. While some oenotheras spread aggressively by underground runners or by producing quantities of fertile seed, others are temperamental and live in the garden only a short period. Cultural requirements for all the perennial species discussed here are the same, loamy soil with good drainage and full sun.

O. berlandieri. MEXICAN EVENING PRIMROSE. Native to Texas and Mexico, this plant was re-introduced to gardeners in our area by Saratoga Horticultural Foundation in the mid-70's. When established, it spreads rapidly on underground runners, a trait that can be an advantage or disadvantage. Planted with *Ceanothus* 'Dark Star' or *Salvia mellifera* 'Terra Seca', its wandering habit would be of value. This cheery day-blooming plant with open, single, pink flowers will light up the garden, May into June. Flowering stems are ordinarily 8 to 10 in. tall, but can grow taller. Cut back severely after bloom. Recently a selection, 'Siskiyou', was introduced by Siskiyou Rare Plant Nursery. It has the same characteristics as *O. berlandieri* except that it is shorter and more clumping.

O. cheiranthifolia. BEACH PRIMROSE. This native to our coastal area has a prostrate habit and wiry stems. The gray foliage is handsome and is set off by day-blooming flowers of butter-yellow that fade to soft orange-red. Quick drainage is a necessity. With its interesting growth habit and summertime flowers, it is a fine choice for the rock garden.

O. hookeri. Evening flowering, this conspicuous plant is found in the Santa Cruz mountains and other places in California. A basal rosette of leaves supports an upright spike of bright yellow flowers 2 to 4 ft. tall. Plants set quantities of fertile seed and can become a nuisance unless grown in rough areas away from borders. A similar species which arose in cultivation is *O. erythrosepala.* Easily grown from seed, it too can become a pest.

O. missourensis. This decumbent, evening-flowering perennial demands space and deserves it! It is a handsome plant with huge mid-yellow flowers that turn red with age. There is a very long summer blooming period. Allow at least three feet for its development and be ready to guide its stems along a path or in front of a border. Unfortunately, it is short-lived. Good drainage may extend its life.

O. odorata. From South America comes this evening-flowering perennial that has a basal rosette of leaves and an ascending flowering stem that reaches 1 to 2 ft. Flowers are a pale yellow and the stem a soft red making a nice association with the green-gray leaves. Again, there is the problem of lots of fertile seed and the foliage is prone to mildew.

O. perennis. SUNDROPS. A saucy little day-flowering sundrop from eastern North America, its foliage is dark green and the plant usually stays under 4 in. Introduced to cultivation in 1757, its small, bright yellow flowers have given sparkle along pathways and between stepping stones for many years. Easily grown from seed.

B.C.

Oenothera berlandieri 'Siskiyou'

ORIGANUM. *Lamiaceae (Labiatae)*. While there are a number of oreganos native to the Mediterranean area, the ones listed here are those most popular as ornamentals for the border and rock garden. These are all herbaceous perennials or sub-shrubs, and are easy to root from cuttings of new growth taken before flowering. All have tightly clustered bracts which resemble hops. Tiny tubular flowers peep from the bracts. Seed may be sown, but may not come true to type when taken from garden plants. The old stems should be cut back to the soil after flowering. All species require full sun and good drainage.

    O. dictamnus. DITTANY OF CRETE. One of the first ornamental oreganos to be grown in the Bay Area, this dwarf shrub was listed in Victor Reiter's first catalog over forty years ago. It is noted for the broad, furry, silver foliage on arching stems which carry the pink bracts and flowers in late summer and fall. It is an excellent plant for a hanging basket.

Origanum x 'Kent Beauty'

O. x 'Kent Beauty'. This English cross is very popular as a pot plant and in the rock garden. The flowering stems are branched with up to 12 bracts on each 12 in. stem. The bracts are pale green fading to pink.

O. libanoticum. The foot-long flowering stems carry the longest bract clusters of the genus, just a little over 4 in. Though rather narrow, these clusters dangle from the tips of the arching stems to make a wonderful show in the garden or basket.

O. microphyllum. This wiry sub-shrub must inhabit the hottest, driest rocks of Crete, judging from the thin purple stems and tiny leaves. The 1 ft. tall, rather upright branches carry few leaves and none toward the end of the stems where bright green bracts hold tiny pink to purple flowers. When in full bloom, there appears to be a pink haze over the entire plant.

O. rotundifolium. This compact grower from Turkey has the largest bracts, very pale green, at the tips of every stem. Light pink flowers tucked inside the bracts make this a stand-out when in full bloom.

O. vulgare 'Aureum'. This is a multi-stem, clump-forming plant with golden yellow foliage. It can be used as an edging or spot of color in the border. It is probably best without reflected heat or very hot sun. Some English authors say this can be used in cooking, and the species is often referred to as "Wild Marjoram".

E.C.

P

PENSTEMON. *Scrophulariaceae*. BEARD TONGUE. This fascinating genus of about 270 perennial species, all but one of them native to North America, is especially abundant in the West. Penstemons vary from mat-forming, rock garden species to 4-5 ft. tall, showy, clump-forming specimens. The tubular flowers are two-lipped and are arranged in numerous pairs or groups of pairs close to the stems. Some species have fairly small flowers, but many have large, lovely ones, the fifth stamen variously bearded (hence the common name), and the corolla often dramatically marked with guide lines that point bees toward nectar and pollen. The blooms are colorful, from deep blue or purple, through brilliant reds, deep to light pinks, lavenders, and into whites. Some are even fragrant. Penstemons bloom over long periods of time and are excellent cut flowers, though some species need to have the cut ends of the stems singed. The leaves are opposite and in many species are handsome. They vary from about 1 to 3 or 4 in. in length. The edges may be entire to variously toothed, the upper ones often joined around the stem. Most species want full sun, and all require good drainage. Natives do especially well on scree slopes, the soil mostly sandy gravel, with restrained watering. Penstemons, though perennial, may be some-what short-lived (3-5 years). Soft wood cuttings are very successful for propagation, and in the fall you may find branches which have layered. They are prolific seed producers and grow easily from seed, but be sure the soil in the seed flat is at least half sand.

P. barbatus. This red-flowering native produces its bloom in early summer. The plants are tall and sprawling so need to be staked or grown among shrubs for support. Several cultivars are available. 'Prairie Fire' has orange-red flowers. 'Rose Elf' is more compact, 12-18 in., with rose-colored flowers.

P. campanulatus. This is one of my most successful natives. It produces many slender but very leafy branches, each ending in several inches of pinky-lavender or lavender-blue flowers, blooming mid-summer and re-blooming if snipped back.

P. gloxiniodes. This large-flowered species is the one most often available in the nurseries and is often called "Garden Penstemon". There are many named cultivars: 'Midnight' (deep purple), 'Huntington Pink', 'Holly's White' among others. These form big clumps of 2-4 ft. stems with deep green leaves. They will bloom from spring through fall if the withered stalks are cut back about 3-4 in. below the lowest flowers. Then usually two new side branches will develop from the leaf axils and rapidly produce buds.

branches will develop from the leaf axils and rapidly produce buds. This is also true of many of the "wild" species, though not all will re-bloom.

P. heterophyllus. Usually labeled 'Blue Bedder', this very successful species is readily available. Low upright or spreading, its woody stems support a fine display of lavender-blue to deep blue flowers, April to July. It is native to the Coastal and Sierran foothills – you ought to see it on Mt. Hamilton. It reseeds easily and is excellent for edges, above walls, and as a colorful pot plant.

P. hirsutus. On my hillside this is a profuse bloomer. It grows to 3 ft. with somewhat hairy leaves and light lavender flowers which reseed generously. For a rock garden, look for 'Pygmaeus'.

P. pseudospectabilis. From the deserts comes this short-lived, but fabulous penstemon. It wants only minimum water and rewards with deep green, attractive leaves, large lavender-blue flowers, and a regular reseeding.

The Penstemon Society annually sends out 2-4 pages listing seeds available at a very modest cost. Many are very easily grown, but do not like to be transplanted even into 6 packs or 2 in. pots until they have several pairs of leaves. Plants of the "wild" species are often available at native plant nurseries such as Yerba Buena.

M.C.

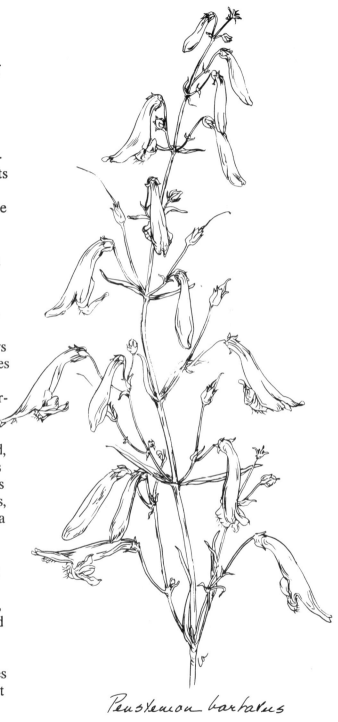

Penstemon barbatus

PEROVSKIA atriplicifolia. *Lamiaceae. (Labiatae).* RUSSIAN SAGE. Not a true sage, nor even Russian, this decorative, ornamental shrub from Pakistan grows to 4 ft. tall and as wide. With drastic pruning it becomes a many-stemmed sub-shrub, though it may be cut back less if the white of the winter stems is to be enjoyed. The flowering stems are thought to resemble the herb lavender, but the placement of the flowers on the stem is more open and the color brighter and bluer. Bloom is in late summer with many spikes developing over several months. The deciduous leaves are grayish-white on the undersides and with the lavender-blue flowers the plant adds a spot of soft lavender-gray to the mixed border. Sun is needed for full bloom. The soil should be on the dry side and good drainage is required. Propagation is by cuttings.

Perovskia is an excellent foil for plants with reddish foliage as well as green. It combines well with other shrubs and with perennials such as baptisia or penstemon.

E.B.

PHLOMIS. *Lamiaceae. (Labiatae).* JERUSALEM SAGE.

P. fruticosa. A shrubby perennial, Jerusalem sage makes a woody- stemmed bush 4 by 3 ft. It will grow in completely dry soil once established and should be combined with plants liking the same dry conditions, such as red-hot pokers and gaillardias. The leaves are almost triangular in shape, rough and wrinkly, greenish-gray. The flowers, appearing from spring through summer, are yellow, although some forms are white-lipped. They are set in plump whorls, 4 in. across along the upper part of the stems. As they fade they should be cut back to encourage more blossoms. In the fall, to keep the plant from becoming rangy, cut it back by about a third to leaf nodes.

P. lanata. A smaller version of Jerusalem sage, this plant grows only 3 ft. tall, with roundish, yellow-green, felted leaves. The flowers are golden yellow, much like their larger counterpart but in whorls under 2 in. at the tips of branches. If they are not cut, new growth will appear beyond them; cutting back to leaf nodes will encourage branching and a fuller plant.

M.V.

PHYSOSTEGIA virginiana. *Lamiaceae. (Labiatae).* OBEDIENCE PLANT, FALSE DRAGONHEAD. This is a lovely background plant. It grows to 4 ft. and will need some staking. Its blossom spikes are as long as 10 in., appearing in late summer. They make excellent cut flowers. The particular plant I have is probably the species, a warm, glowing pink. I say "probably the species" because I got it from a neighbor, formerly of Virginia. That clump, or some part of it is now in its third garden. First, it backed a late-blooming bronzy hemerocallis – that was a sight! Next, it was in a garden where the soil was below the poverty level and water was at a minimum. The plant looked wimpy, but it sent up foot-high stalks of bloom. Now it is in a good place with fairly rich soil, and as much water as conscience will allow. It is shooting up its light, bright green leaves and will bloom along with low-growing *Aster alpinus* and tall-growing *A. nova-belgii* – my mauve decade corner, I call it.

This plant needs fairly good soil and regular water. It goes completely dormant for a while in winter leaving dry stems unless you cut them off, and they are not pretty. The bright green of new growth starts early in the spring. There are two cultivars mentioned in the literature, 'Vivida', a rosy pink, and 'Summer Snow', described as least invasive. *P. virginiana* is certainly a spreader, but that allows you to be generous with your divisions.
M.G.

Physostegia virginiana

PLATYCODON grandiflorus. *Campanulaceae.* BALLOON FLOWER. This amusing balloon-shaped, blue flower from east Asia always catches the attention of passers-by. The balloon shape is caused by the fusing of the petals as they emerge from the bud, though most varieties will go on to open out into the large 2 in. wide star-shaped bells of the campanulas. The flowers are usually blue but may also be pink or white. Plant in a sunny location with only a moderate amount of water; it is easy to overwater in a container. Start seed in the spring, set out in the summer in its permanent location, and expect flowers in two years. Plants will grow to 3 ft. tall, though usually less. Bloom is in summer. The plants die to the ground in winter, so be sure you have marked their location. Established plants can be divided, but the clumps must not be allowed to dry out. Var. *mariesii* is shorter, to 1-1/2 ft. high. In 'Komachi' the flowers maintain the balloon shape and never fully open.

B.Y.

POTENTILLA. *Rosaceae.* CINQUEFOIL. Potentilla is a large genus of annuals, perennials, and shrubs of wide distribution in the northern hemisphere, mainly in mountainous or far northern climates, giving them a high degree of toughness and hardiness. The common name, "Cinquefoil", means five-leaved, actually five leaflets arranged palmately. The leaflets are usually toothed and are more or less hairy, according to species.

P. nepalensis 'Miss Willmott'. An evergreen perennial from the Himalayas, this cultivar was named for Miss Ellen Willmott, a famous English gardener. It grows in a congested, spreading, even rather sprawling, but attractive mat, about two feet across. The flowering stems reach out horizontally a foot longer, branching at the ends where the flowers are borne. The flowers are five-petalled and rose-like, the color unique, deep rose in the center shading to salmon at the edges. It is not really a profuse bloomer but a steady one, from early summer well into fall. Give it full sun and either keep it a little on the dry side or make sure it has good drainage. It seems to be without many insect pests and to be perfectly hardy.

P. recta. From the Mediterranean region with the usual potentilla foliage, this evergreen species grows more upright than the preceding, with its flowering stems held well above the foliage. The flowers are bright yellow, and while each flush of bloom doesn't last very long, the plant will repeat bloom if dead-headed. *P. recta* is a bit coarse and it does seed about prolifically, but it is tough and drought resistant and contributes its cheerful color and handsome foliage for very little fuss on the gardener's part.

P. tabernaemontana *(P. verna).* A low, creeping, evergreen species used as a ground cover with the typical five-parted foliage and bright yellow flowers. From the original small 6 in. high clump it throws out its long stems, rooting as it goes, strawberry fashion, and spreads very quickly. As a ground cover, it fills in and blooms best in full sun with adequate water, but it will grow in part shade (or practically anywhere else) once it gets started. One should think carefully before planting this one, because it is extremely hard to eradicate once it is established, especially in a mixed flower bed. The ideal site is an open space defined by some effective barriers where it will not get much foot traffic. For such a location it can be very handsome and satisfactory.

E.C.G.

RANUNCULUS. *Ranunculaceae.* BUTTERCUP.

R. cortusaefolius. From Tenerife, this is probably the largest of the genus used in the garden. The broad basal leaves are almost round with scalloped edges. The elegant, shiny, butter-yellow flowers are held erect in broad sprays on 2 to 3 ft. stems. Spring flowering, this plant is summer dormant, so can be left without water till the winter rains begin in the fall. Grow it from seed.

R. repens 'Pleniflorus'. CREEPING BUTTERCUP. This rampant creeper has dark green leaves and small, double, yellow flowers. It requires regular watering. Rooting at every node, this is best used as a ground cover where it can have freedom to roam.

E.C.

Ranunculus cortusaefolius

REHMANNIA elata. *Scrophulariaceae.* From China comes this lovely perennial. Its foxglove-like, 2 to 3 in. tubular flowers are loosely set on 2 to 3 ft. stems, usually in a rosy purple with yellow and red throat markings. There is also a less commonly seen creamy-white variety. The bloom period is long, from early summer until the cold of late autumn. It spreads by underground roots, though is not at all invasive, and makes a large clump of evergreen, coarse-toothed leaves. The plants are most successful in good soil, with ample water, and in partial shade, such as under tall shrubs or trees. Propagation is by cuttings or division.

I have had two plantings, the first petered out after several years, but I have obtained both the rosy-purple and the creamy-white again and they are vigorous after a year of growth placed under a fence-trained, arching Banksia rose, facing southeast. Too much shade prevents a healthy, long blooming period. My plants were obtained at Strybing Arboretum and at the Western Horticultural Society's plant table.

S.B.

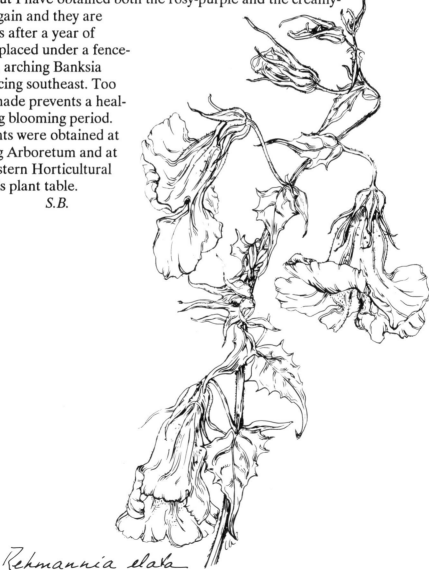

Rehmannia elata

ROMNEYA coulteri. *Papaveraceae.* MATILIJA POPPY, FRIED EGG PLANT, TREE POPPY. Unarguably the most beautiful California native perennial, *Romneya* is also one of the largest and most aggressive. It grows to 10 ft. tall and spreads underground to form large colonies. In general, the heavier the soil, the slower it spreads.

The foliage and stems are a beautiful, glaucous, blue-gray color. Early in the season, as the new stems and leaves expand, you might even think that the foliage alone was reason enough to grow this plant, but you would be wrong, because shortly after the stems have reached their full height in May or June, spectacular 6 to 10 in. diameter, white, crepe-like flowers with a giant boss of golden stamens appear in great quantity. The flowers have the very pleasant fragrance of ripe apricots and are showy cut flowers.

The most difficult aspect of cultivating the Matilija poppy is getting it established. Full sun, sloped land, excellent drainage, and a poor soil are preferred by this plant, although they can be grown just about anywhere as long as they are in the sun and do not get too much water. Excess water, especially in the summer will cause the plant to rot. *Romneya* is also an excellent plant for erosion control. Cut all the stems back to 3 or 4 in. stubs some time between November and January, before the new growth gets underway. The plants will respond with lush new growth and many more flowers. Use the Matilija poppy with other rugged plants like salvias, phlomis, eriogonums, and bold bunch grasses.

B.O'B.

ROSMARINUS. *Lamiaceae. (Labiatae).* ROSEMARY. For over 2300 years people have treasured the heady fragrance of rosemary and grown it for its medicinal virtues and culinary uses, as well as for symbolic and poetic associations. "Dew of the sea" is the meaning of its ancient Latin name and proclaims its home to be seaside habitats, tolerating wind, salt spray, sandy soils, and little rain. If planted in heavy soil in a conventional garden, it tends to build up wood quickly. Placed in full sun with quick drainage, its seaside conditions can be imitated. Sir Thomas More wrote, "As for rosemary I let it run all over my garden walls, not only because my bees love it, but because it is the herb sacred to remembrance and to friendship, whence a sprig of it hath a dumb language." Surely his garden walls were bathed in full sunlight, his soil fast-draining, and his air able to move rapidly and sweetly with the perfume of his revered rosemary.

Here in California where deer can be a problem, there is conflicting evidence as to whether rosemaries are plants that deer seem to avoid. Some herds regularly find, then nip all the new growth of all the rosemary cultivars discussed here. Other herds, apparently, don't even bother to taste old or new growth in unprotected plantings. It would seem to be strictly a matter of luck!

The following list of cultivars would make suitable selections for a Mediterranean garden or a dry section of a cottage garden. Blooming occurs during prolonged warm spells from late fall through spring. Hillside gardens featuring artemisia, grevillea, lavender, helichrysum, and rosemary would combine plants that require the same cultural conditions, but allow a wide and varied range of foliage, textures, and flower color.

'Albus' is a near-white flowering form that has an erect habit. Reaching 3 ft. in height and 2 ft. in width, it is multi- stemmed with broad, yellow-green leaves spaced airily on the stems. It flowers from late winter into spring. An interesting combination would be to grow it with a native California sage, *Salvia sonomensis.* The strong green, broad-leaved sage would be in harmonious opposition to the narrow-leaved 'Albus'. Blooming periods, unfortunately, do not overlap.

'Benenden Blue' has remarkably thin and fine foliage and will attain 4 or 5 ft. after a number of years. It has a somewhat twisted appearance as well as a sparsely clothed one, due to the thin, needle-like leaves. The foliage is pine-scented, and the flowers dark violet-blue. The interesting foliage and large, though sparse, flowers would be admirably shown grown next to *Lavandula* x *intermedia* 'Provence'.

'Blue Spire', a cultivar originally from England, is slow-growing and in time will make a fine upright plant about 4 by 4 ft. Its leaves are dull yellow-green, of medium width, and more or less evenly spaced on the stem. Cornflower-blue flowers are plentiful, usually occurring in late winter or early spring. A fine plant for adding stature and background to a dry border.

'Collingwood Ingram', with dark green and glossy leaves, will reach about 3 to 4 ft. in height, then build on arching stems 3 ft. across. Attracting bees and insects, its flowers are an intense blue and do not fade in strong sunlight. Planted with *Lavandula dentata candicans*, its dark foliage makes a rich contrast with the gray-green foliage of the lavender.

'Ken Taylor' is a sport of 'Collingwood Ingram' and was recognized by Elizabeth de Forest when she visited the garden of the nurseryman whose name it bears in Aromas, California. Recently it has been given wider distribution by Saratoga Horticultural Foundation. This is an outstanding cultivar for several reasons. The intense violet-blue flowers are set off by wide, dark green foliage. The habit of the plant is more prostrate than that of 'Collingwood Ingram' and makes for a flatter, more trailing plant. Less than 2 ft. tall and more than that wide, its growth habit commends it for wall plantings where it could trail and spill with grace and charm.

'Lockwood de Forest' occurred as a chance seedling in the de Forest garden in Santa Barbara in the 1940's. With deep green leaves and pale blue flowers its habit is prostrate but mounding about 1-1/2 ft. off the ground and spreading 2 to 3 ft. Although widely used as a ground cover, this is perhaps not its best function, for its growth is not thick and heavy enough to keep weeds from seeding throughout plantings. However, situated in the front of borders or along paths or walkways, it would admirably soften edges and could be combined with the thickly growing, dark green-leaved *Teucrium chamaedrys*.

'Majorca Pink' grows about 3 to 4 ft. tall, making long arching stems. The narrow leaves are a yellow-green and look neat and tidy on the curving stems. The oils in the leaves are strongly aromatic. This plant is not a shy bloomer but throws pinkish-lavender flowers throughout the winter months, a good plant for containers or dry border.

'Miss Jessupp's Upright' is an English cultivar recognized by E.A.Bowles and named for his gardening friend, Miss Euphema Jessupp. It was introduced to California in 1957 from Sissinghurst Castle by Elizabeth de Forest. As if the above mentioned people and places aren't enough to make one want to grow the plant for the illustrious company it keeps, listen to its botanical attributes! It is a sturdy, upright shrub, reaching about 6 ft. in height and 4 ft. across with wide yellow-green leaves, glossy and highly fragrant, that can be used culinarily as well as in potpourri. Flowers are a pale, but lively blue. This plant makes an excellent hedge and will fill in more tightly with light shearing and shaping, fine for a windscreen.

'Pine-scented' rosemary is a small, airy shrub under 4 ft. tall and up to 2 ft. across. It has a strong pine odor when its thin, medium-green leaves are brushed. Very slow growing with mid-blue flowers, it would do well in containers.

'Tuscan Blue' can be found in nurseries from the East to the West Coast, but at present it is doubtful that the true cultivar is obtainable in this country. 'Tuscan Blue' was originally observed in Tuscany where it was and is widely used as a hedging plant. W. Arnold Forster of Cornwall recognized its merits and introduced it into English cultivation. His selection is upright in habit with broad and glossy medium-green leaves that are very aromatic and are enhanced by ceanothus-blue flowers. This tender plant has succeeded in only the mildest parts of England, but should do well in our moderate climate if only we could find it. What is sold here as 'Tuscan Blue' does flourish, whether the true cultivar or not.

B.C.

RUTA graveolens. *Rutaceae.* HERB-OF-GRACE, RUE. It is easy to find literary allusions to this herb. It is more difficult to find an herbal use for it. In the garden, however, its foliage can provide a texture and color that not only please in themselves, but also fit well in a group of gray-green plants. Though it may grow to 2 or 3 ft., mine stays less than 18 in. tall with a broader spread. The leaves of 'Jackman's Blue', probably the best variety, are a fine blue-gray. Viewed closely, they are like those of a small maidenhair fern, but the total effect of the plant is a billow of smoky gray-green. The flowers are an insignificant yellow. The seed pods are reputed to be interesting, but my plant has never produced any. Some people's skin is sensitive to the plant, but since it requires little care, the problem may be minor, and since the scent of the crushed leaf is not pleasant, one is not tempted to do more than admire the appearance. Good garden soil on the alkaline side with sun and average to little water should keep the plant healthy. I group mine with lavender and santolina with some red or blue flowers for contrast. Propagation is by seed or cuttings.

K.B.

S

SALVIA. *Lamiaceae. (Labiatae).* SAGE. The name is from the Latin *salvus*, meaning safe, well, sound, from the medicinal use of some of the species. This genus of 700 to 900 species occurs throughout the temperate and subtropical regions of the world. The number of species is so vast that botanists are still in the process of collecting and describing individuals in specific geographical areas. Gardeners may be interested to know that cultural requirements of salvias run the gamut from full sun to shade, light to heavy watering, clay to gravelly or sandy soil, and some have no toleration for wind. The selection described here was made on the basis of color of flower and height of plant. All are easily combined with other plants in a Bay Area border, taking into consideration cultural information given.

S. argentea. The specific name describes the leaves, silvery. This biennial/perennial is easily grown from seed and can be encouraged to persist by removing the flowering stalk before it sets seed. Once in awhile let the seed self-sow in order to have young plants to move about. The foliage is perfectly marvelous to observe; in summer the plant is tiny, establishing its roots, then when fall comes the leaves take off in growth, elongating by mid-winter to two feet. The leaves have been called "gray plush" because of the white woolly texture. Do watch for snails and slugs under such an ample surface. Blooming occurs sporadically throughout mild periods beginning in spring. The 3 ft. stem of white flowers blushed pinkish-lavender may be used in an arrangement. This salvia should be planted at the edge of a border in order to give the leaves plenty of space to develop and be seen. Situate in light clay soil, full sun, and give moderate to light waterings.

S. elegans. 'Honeymelon' is a delightful selection of the good old standby, pineapple sage. It grows to about 1 ft. in height and spreads on underground runners. The foliage when brushed has the same fruity odor as the species. Try planting it in front of an evergreen shrub such as our native *Galvezia speciosa* for the scarlet red blossoms of both plants make quite a nice effect. 'Honeymelon' is apparently evergreen in this climate and free flowering, throwing blossoms throughout the growing season. It is handsome poking in and out of any of the small-growing, white daisies such as *Anthemis tinctoria* 'E.C.Buxton' or *Chrysanthemum frutescens* 'White Lady'. Clay soil with dressings of compost, moderate watering, and a good half-day of sun are suggested.

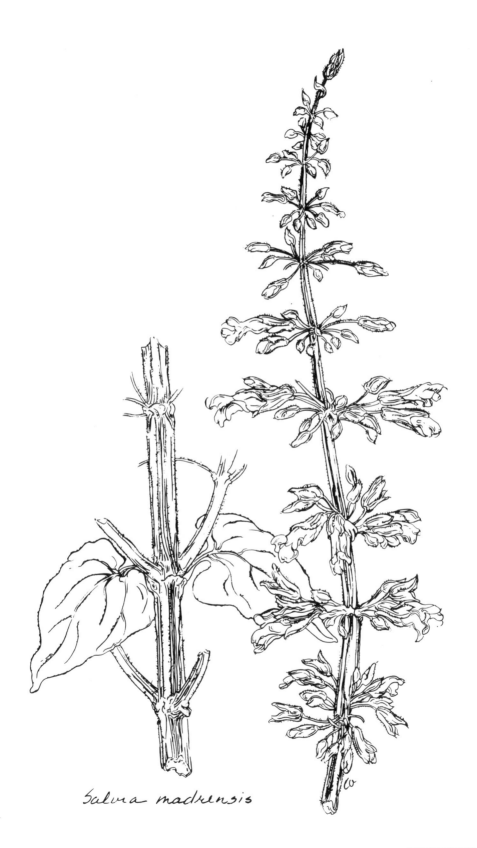

Salvia madrensis

S. guaranitica. From Brazil, Paraguay, and Argentina comes this colonizing sub-shrub. It is sometimes called anise scented because of the odor given from bruised leaves, but this attribute is ephemeral and not always detectable. Five-foot tall upright stems carry yellow-green leaves which make a fine pool of color from spring until frost. The leaves give a sparkling effect on either sunny or overcast days, probably because their surface is smooth. The first of July usually marks the beginning of the flowering season. From then until frost, truly blue flowers will be ever-present in a mass of plants. The plant spreads by underground runners, but the colony can easily be controlled to any desired space by simply pulling out and discarding wanderers. Incidentally, there are nodules on the roots that look like little fat finger-like appendages similar to nitrogen fixers on other plants. Flowers do not last long in arrangements. Moderately heavy soil, full sun, and light watering will produce continual bloom. Cut plants to the ground after frost. They deserve a rest! A red rose bush or red dahlias would make remarkably fine companions.

S. madrensis. This fine fall-into-winter-blooming sage has only recently been grown and distributed as a garden subject. To my best knowledge it was collected by a staff expedition of the Huntington Botanic Garden to the Sierra Madre in Mexico in 1977. Most likely all material grown in this area has come from cuttings of a plant grown from seed collected on that expedition. This is a very stout 5 ft. tall plant with such beautiful square stems it would be worth growing for that character alone. In September or October the flowering season begins,and whorls of soft yellow blossoms appear. The inflorescence is sticky, but not the other parts of the plant. Heart-shaped, mid-green leaves of various sizes add their special interest. This salvia is a colonizer, and if possible, enough space should be allowed for it to make a large patch. Moderately heavy soil and shade from either adjoining plants or tall trees are a must for good performance. Light summer watering is needed. Cut canes to the ground and remove dead leaves in February. A large viburnum or buddleia would make a good companion.

S. patens. GENTIAN SAGE. Grown and loved since its introduction in 1838, this salvia is sometimes called the gentian sage because of the true-blue color of its flowers. A compact plant, it grows about 1 to 1-1/2 ft. tall and 1 ft. wide. Often treated as an annual, it is popular as a bedding-out plant, but in this area you will find that it will exhibit its perennial qualities and persist for years with a bit of care. Medium heavy soil, full sun, and good drainage are musts. Liberal fertilizing and watering are needed for repeat bloom. After the initial bloom, shear all flowering stalks, then feed and water well. In a long, cool summer you may get four flowerings. Its apple-green leaves look nice with smallish gray foliage plants such as *Artemisia pontica.* Or consider a blue and red flower combination, red petunias and *Berberis thunbergii* 'Atropurpurea' are possibilities.

S. spathacea. PITCHER SAGE. One of many fine native plants of California, this species has been in cultivation for over a hundred years. A robust perennial with creeping rhizomes forming mat-like clumps, it blooms several times during the growing season. The foliage is more or less evergreen, the leaf shaped like a broad-nosed arrowhead and very hairy. There are many glands on all parts of the plant, that when brushed release a fruity odor. The inflorescence reaches over a foot in height and the calyx is as colorful as the flowers, a rich, wine red. In the wild it is found at the edge of forests growing in deep humus. Situate the plant in full sun or high shade in medium clay soil with a yearly dressing of compost and it will do well in your garden. No extra water is needed unless there is a prolonged hot spell. The flowering spikes would have a fine background if planted in front of an evergreen shrub such as coffeeberry, *Rhamnus californica*, and the cultural requirements would be similar. *Salvia sonomensis* would also be a good companion.

B.C.

SANTOLINA. *Asteraceae. (Compositae).*

S. chamaecyparissus. LAVENDER COTTON. This is one of the best of the "silvers" for its toughness and neatness. It can be clipped into a low hedge or edging or into a rounded dome to add a sculptural element to the border and a cooling foil to bright colors. A 2 ft. sub-shrub, it is woody at base, much branched and densely clothed with tiny, four-ranked, toothed gray leaves that look like miniature cypress foliage. It will become sprawling and woody if left unpruned but is relatively easy to control with an annual winter clipping. The button-like, bright yellow flowers are best removed if a trim, formal shape is desired. Santolina is a very tough and hardy plant. Give it full sun, poor soil, little water, and, once established, it will need little care. There is a dwarf cultivar with even smaller foliage that is used in knot gardens and edgings.

S. virens. The bright green leaves are longer and narrower than those of *S. chamaecyparissus* and give the plant a softer, looser look. The two species are very effective planted together. The flowers of *S. virens* are creamy yellow buttons and are so attractive with the green foliage that it is hard to bring oneself to trim them off as one should do to keep the plant in shape. *S. virens* is less rugged than its gray-leaved cousin. It needs more water in the summer, though it is by no means a thirsty plant, otherwise the culture is the same. Both are easy to propagate from cuttings, and both are strongly aromatic.

E.C.G.

SAPONARIA. *Caryophyllaceae.* SOAPWORT.

S. ocymoides. Soapwort comes from the Mediterranean, a good clue that it will do well here. It grows 1 ft. tall with a sprawling habit to 3 ft. wide and likes to spill over rocks or grow at the top of a wall. The leaves are small and dark green. The pink flowers are about 1 in. across and cover the plant in profusion in early summer. There are also white forms, so it is best to propagate this plant from cuttings, as the seedlings (many) are quite variable. Be sure to cut it back after flowering to keep it compact. Any soil is suitable. Plenty of sun and average water (even a certain amount of drought) will keep this plant happy.

S. pumila. Low-growing and very compact, this plant appears to be one which would root easily because of its close contact with the soil, but the opposite is true. Though only 1 in. tall by 8 in. wide, it has a tap root, which may explain why it does so well in adverse conditions. Plants in my garden have managed to look good all year in spite of neglect, very little water, scorching sun, and poor soil. In spring they reward me for this treatment with a lovely display of seemingly oversized, pink, tubular flowers about 1 in. in length. The dried flowers remain on the plant for some time and may need to be physically removed by brushing them off. The leaves are tiny and bright green.

Plants which combine well with this native of the Carpathian mountains are *Achillea ageratifolia, Dianthus deltoides,* and other small rock garden plants that won't overrun it.

M.K.

SATUREJA montana. *Lamiaceae. (Labiatae).* WINTER SAVORY. This pungent herb looks best in a sunny rock garden. It is a sub-shrub, no more than 12 in. tall, with a woody inner structure that is covered in summer with white or pink flowers, busy with bees. The 1 in. long, dark green, linear leaves persist through the year and are best sheared for drying before the flowers appear. In the fall another grooming will keep the plant neat and ready for a burst of spring growth. This species is from the Mediterranean and does best in full sun. With good drainage the plant will accept average garden water, but will also do well in a drier situation. Propagation is by seed (often self-sown), by cuttings, or by division.

K.B.

SCAEVOLA 'Mauve Clusters'. *Goodeniaceae.* FAIRY FAN FLOWER. Native to Australia, this prostrate ground cover becomes a dense mat 4 in. high, reaching 4 to 5 ft. in width. Light mauve, fan-shaped flowers cover the bright green leaves from spring into fall. It grows in full sun or partial shade and requires some summer water. I water my plant about every two weeks in hot weather. The long blooming period and unusual flower shape make this plant an inter-

Scaevola 'Mauve Clusters'

esting addition to the garden. It is usually available at Santa Cruz Arboretum, and I have also seen it offered at several local nurseries. Once you have it, propagation by division is easy. Scaevola combines well with low, dainty plants such as *Gypsophila repens* 'Rosea', dwarf sea lavender, and *Incarvillea arguta*, a new arrival on the local market.

D. D.

SENECIO. *Asteraceae. (Compositae).* Senecios comprise an enormous genus of over 2,000 species that include cactus-like and fleshy succulents, vines, and shrubs as well as herbaceous annuals and perennials. They are generally of easy culture, although they may be tender to frost. Velvety, gray-foliaged varieties will tolerate ordinary soil as long as drainage is good and can survive with almost no water during our rainless months. Like other gray or white-leaved plants, they have a luminous quality that helps to show the way along a path or driveway at night.

S. cineraria. DUSTY MILLER. The dusty millers, sometimes called *Cineraria maritima*, perhaps because of their Mediterranean provenance, are grown for their silvery-white, woolly foliage rather than their flowers, which are nearly rayless clusters of yellow or cream of no particular value either in the garden or for cutting. When blooming starts, the plants quickly become woody and leggy, so at this time it is wise to cut them back to keep fresh foliage coming on strongly. Seed is available for the better cultivars, such as 'Cirrus' and 'Silver Dust', and, during summer, plants are readily available in nurseries. If you have a source of plants, you can easily start them from cuttings at almost any time. Every two or three years it would be well to start with new plants rather than continually cutting back. Grow them in full sun or with only the least amount of shade. Dusty millers are traditionally used in beds with pastel blue and pink flowers and especially in rose gardens, but they also help to cool combinations of hot yellow, orange, and red flowers such as salvias and zinnias.

S. vira-vira. *(S. leucostachys).* With leaves that are almost bone white, this Argentine species must be one of the whitest plants in existence, and its several narrow lobes, cutting almost to the center of the leaf, make the leaves look like fish skeletons. The stems like to trail up, over, and through nearby plants or to curve loosely outward, rooting wherever they touch the ground. If you have a large bank to cover, this might be what you would like the plant to do, but it can be confined and forced to grow upright by severely pruning it at regular intervals. A good time to start pruning is in summer after the creamy white clusters of fluffy blossoms darken to reddish brown.

This is a shrubby perennial, useful in a border with other gray and greenish-gray plants such as *Helichrysum petiolatum, Ballota pseudodictamnus,* and perhaps adding for contrast some purple-leaved sage, *Salvia officinalis* 'Purpurea'.

M.V.

SEDUM spectabile. *Crassulaceae.* STONECROP. From China comes this herbaceous sedum with succulent stems and thick, fleshy, almost round-toothed leaves. These can quickly develop into a pleasing clump of gray-green in the summer border. Large flat heads of starry, pink flowers develop in the summer and attract hordes of butterflies and bees well into the fall. It grows best in full sun. Clumps should be divided every two or three years so that they do not become overgrown, otherwise the flower stems fall away from the center of the clump. Good yellow and orange winter color develops as the leaves wither. If the flower stems are left on the plant after the leaves have fallen, they can then be picked for dried arrangements. In the past few years there have been several cultivars of *S. spectabile* available including: 'Brilliant', rose red; 'Carmen', soft pink; 'Meteor', carmine red; 'Stardust', white. 'Autumn Joy', probably a hybrid between *S. spectabile* and *S. telephium,* is very popular and widely available. These will all grow 18 to 24 in. tall and are easy to grow from divisions in the spring. They can be used in the border with almost any combination of perennials and also make excellent pot plants.

E.C.

SIDALCEA malviflora. *Malvaceae.* CHECKERBLOOM. This easily grown California native has evergreen, scalloped, rounded leaves and 1 in., bright pink, hollyhock-like flowers along its 18 in. stems. Checkerbloom is a plant of our coastal hills and can be seen locally in abundance on San Bruno Mountain and along the San Mateo County coastline. The foliage mass is about 4 to 5 in. high and the plants form mats up to 3 ft. across. The flowering stems are usually not held firmly upright, instead they often shoot out at various angles, creating a casual (some would say untidy) effect. Easy to grow in any sunny border, this plant generally prefers a bit of extra water in the summer.

B.O'B.

SILENE. *Caryophilaceae.* CAMPION.

S. virginica. FIRE PINK. Native to eastern and mid-western states south from New Jersey and Minnesota, this campion does well on the Peninsula. It forms a 2 to 3 ft. high mound of deep green, long, narrow, spoon-shaped leaves making a good background for the strikingly vivid, scarlet-red, lacy flowers. The deeply-toothed petals flare above a sticky, glandular calyx, 3/4 to 1 in. long. Culture is the same as for the following.

S. vulgaris ssp. maritima. BLADDER CAMPION, SEA CAMPION. Native to coastal areas from Norway to Spain, this species is tolerant of a

Silene vulgaris ssp. maritima

wide range of temperatures. Forming a mat 6 to 8 in. high with white flowers, it is good in a sunny spot for ground cover or will cascade over a wall or down from a hanging container. The calyx under the petals is inflated like a bladder or balloon. Its 5-petaled flowers are reminiscent of dianthus but the petals are separated by deep lobes. On the Peninsula it blooms from spring till frost. It should be cut back during the winter to renew growth, but then it looks scraggly in winter anyway. Shear back anytime blooming slows down; the plant will respond. Propagate by division in winter or by seed. It is sold in the trade usually as *S. maritima.*

B.Y.

SMILACINA. *Liliaceae.* FALSE SOLOMON'S SEAL. There are two native smilacinas which are very easy to grow under woodland conditions-- shade, some moisture (not too much in summer), good drainage, and a fairly rich organic soil (no heavy clay). These plants have a quiet, delicate charm about them and never really call attention to themselves. Both will form clumps in time, especially *S. stellata,* which can cover large areas under ideal conditions. These plants are deciduous at odd times. *S. racemosa* goes dormant just after the berries have ripened in September/October and comes back again in March/April. *S. stellata* generally vanishes in July/August and returns in February, nearly always before *S. racemosa.* Both species are found in forests or at the edges of forests, with *S. racemosa* usually in habitats a bit drier than those of *S. stellata.* Propagation of both is by division.

 S. racemosa var. amplexicaulis. Much larger than *S. stellata,* this species will form a nice clump about 3 ft. across and about 2 to 3 ft. tall. The stems arch gracefully, and the minute flowers are densely clustered in terminal panicles. The flowers are very fragrant on some plants, have no fragrance on others. If the flowers are pollinated, they form large, showy, red berries that are over 1/8 in. across and last for several weeks before they are eaten by birds or other creatures.

 S. stellata var. sessilifolia. This species is about 8 to 12 in. high and can form broad colonies. The flowers are larger and fewer in number than *S. racemosa* and never make quite the show. I have never noticed berries on this plant, but would expect that it does produce them from time to time. The stems are also arching, but not as much as *S. racemosa*; in fact, *S. stellata* has a more erect habit except for the very tips, which always arch in the same direction.

B.O'B.

STACHYS byzantina. *Lamiaceae. (Labiatae).* LAMB'S EARS. This is probably the best known species of the genus. It is often grown as a border in herb gardens, but it is equally useful in flower beds and makes a wonderful silvery cover for uninteresting bare earth under roses. Its leaves are shaped as much like a rabbit's ears as a lamb's, about 6 in. long, covered with silky hairs that add to the animal-like appearance. They are gray-white. It is for the color and unusual texture of the leaves that we grow the plant, not for its flowers. These are rosy lavender in whorls set above smaller leaves on tall, 8 to 10 in. stalks. Many people find them unattractive and cut them off, but flower arrangers like to dry them. It is an easy plant to grow, asking little but sunshine, no excess water, and good drainage. Drainage is important, as the densely-haired leaves, lying close to the ground and overlapping one another, admit little air to dry the crown, thus inviting rot. The lowest leaves turn mushy and brown during cool, rainy weather and need cleaning up when spring warms the air. That is also a good time to divide the plants. 'Silver Carpet' is a cultivar that scarcely ever blooms and thus is preferred by those who dislike the flowers. Its leaves are a little more refined in their hairiness, but the difference between the two varieties is minor.

M.V.

STOKESIA laevis.

Asteraceae. (Compositae).
STOKES ASTER. In well-drained
soil and full sun this native of
our southeastern states is a
reliable, long-blooming and
easily grown perennial. Sturdy, erect, branching stems to
2 ft. tall bear corymbs of
aster-like flower heads. Each
head is composed of a center
of many, small, close-set, fertile, tubular flowers sur-
rounded by a ring of larger,
strap-shaped, sterile flowers.
The edges of the outer
flowers are 5-lobed, giving
the flower a shaggy ap-
pearance. The basic color is
lavender-blue, but many
named cultivars in white,
purple, rose, and sky-blue are
available. The blue forms
look well with achilleas,
coreopsis, African marigolds,
and other yellow flowers.
Bloom is in the summer and
propagation is by seeds or
division.

E.C.G.

Stokesia laevis

T

TEUCRIUM. *Lamiaceae. (Labiatae).* GERMANDER. The generic name was used by Dioscorides, probably for Teucer, first king of Troy, who used the plant medicinally. There are about 300 species of these herbs, sub-shrubs, and shrubs, and they are widely distributed but mostly in the Mediterranean region. They may be propagated by seed, or in midsummer by cuttings and divisions. All plants discussed here are more or less evergreen and their culture is similar. A gritty soil for fast drainage will encourage good root run. A light dressing of wood chips will keep the surface soil cool. Full sun and moderate to light watering are advised. Members of this genus rarely are bothered by diseases, insects or fungi, and generally look good year round.

T. aroanium. From the mountains of Greece, this delightful small plant makes silvery-leaved clumps about 8 in. high and up to 1 ft. wide. The handsome foliage is aromatic, and the small leaves are precisely arranged in rosettes. Pale pinkish-lavender flowers begin to appear in May and June. Plant it in the garden away from more vigorous plants that might swamp it. It would do well in a sunny trough or rock garden.

T. chamaedrys. WALL GERMANDER. This popular species comes from Europe and southwest Asia. With erect stems, small, dark green leaves, and pert little hot-pink flowers it has been widely used through the centuries as an edging plant. Reaching a little over a foot in height and less in width, it takes shearing readily, making it ideal for knot gardens. Unclipped it would be handsome at the front of a border with gray foliage behind it, such as *Achillea* 'Moonshine' or *Ballota acetabulosa.* All these plants have evergreen leaves. Because of the wall germander's pleasant scent, clippings were long used as a strewing herb and also medicinally for fevers, indigestion, melancholy, and gout. Clearly, not an herb to be without! There is a dwarf form, 'Prostratum', that tends to run wherever it pleases. There is available a variegated foliage form with stripes of green and cream.

T. fruticans. TREE GERMANDER. BUSH GERMANDER. Found throughout southern Europe, this species has been in cultivation since 1869 and with its many attributes should remain in favor for years to come. This shrub with whitish-gray leaves will reach 4 ft. or more in height and in width. It responds well to yearly pruning after bloom. Spikes of pale lavender-blue flowers give a bit of sparkle in early summer and again in fall. It makes a soft spot of color in the herbaceous border, or it might be used with one of the upright, dark rosemaries for contrast. There is a smaller form, *T. f.* 'Nana', that has similar attributes. Layering is the easiest way of propagation.

T. marum. This small shrub has a wide distribution throughout the Mediterranean area. It is called cat thyme and might prove dangerous if situated next to a valuable plant, because some cats do love to roll around in it. Upright in habit with diminutive gray foliage, its perky, little mauve-tinted flowers appear in June. It stays relatively low, less than a foot in height and half that in width, quite a nice choice for the rock garden or containers or in a group near the front of the border.

T. scorodonia. WOOD SAGE. This species is apparently not favored in this area, for it is rarely seen or grown. However, its cultivar 'Crispum' is widely grown and admired. It is a European native with lax foliage reaching a foot in height, that is, if you would hold it up to measure! A rhizomatous plant, it will spread rapidly on underground runners if watered regularly, but by holding to minimal water after the plant is established, its growth can be restricted. Though it will take full sun, it does best in part shade. Never failing to attract attention because of its frilly leaves, it would make a nice groundcover that would hide the bare canes of an old tea rose. The flowers are cream-colored and blend into the foliage. When they appear, it is time to prune very heavily. If this is done before the first of August, there will be fresh, frilly leaves throughout the winter.

B.C.

THALICTRUM. *Ranunculaceae.* MEADOW RUE. Where an effect of height without weight is wanted in the perennial border, thalictrums are the ideal choice. Standing 3 to 8 ft. high, according to species, with foliage that resembles columbine or maidenhair fern, they have an airy delicacy that belies their hardiness. Because they are completely herbaceous, the whole plant is renewed each year, giving the pale green or blue-green foliage a special freshness, and one that is seldom marred by insect damage. In nature they are usually found in moist open meadows in full sun, but garden conditions suit them perfectly well, and in our hot, dry climate they appreciate partial shade where their cool, ferny appearance seems especially appropriate. Our native species, in fact, prefer some shade. Some species of thalictrums bear male and female flowers on separate plants, the male flowers usually being the more showy by virtue of

Thalictrum dipterocarpum

the elongate, sometimes colored brush of stamens. There are no petals, but the sepals are often colored. The flowers are small but numerous, charming rather than showy, the chief beauty of the plant being its foliage. Propagation is usually by division or by seed sown in the fall.

T. aquilegifolium. Its columbine-like foliage gives this plant its specific name. This species makes a 3 ft. by 1 ft. clump of blue-green compound leaves, each division bearing three roundish three-lobed leaflets. Fluffy flowers are borne on the ends of the stems in many branched heads. There are several forms, whose flowers may be purple, white, or yellow. Height may also vary among cultivars.

T. dipterocarpum. This most elegant and stately species comes from China and may reach 5 ft. or more. The plant is more open and branching and the foliage finer than *T. aquilegifolium* and more ferny. The flowers are carried in wide, airy panicles, the sepals, usually purple, enclosing a tuft of cream-colored stamens. Before opening, the buds are tiny perfect spheres like drops of water. There is also a white form, 'Album', and a double purple, 'Hewitt's Double', though the latter is not as hardy or as tall as the species. Height depends, in part, on the richness of the soil and the available moisture. At the edge of a lawn at Filoli, there is a splendid specimen that tops 8 ft. each year.

T. polycarpum. This native California species is well worth growing for its delicate and graceful foliage. The compound leaves are gray-green, the individual leaflets fan-shaped and scalloped. Since this species lives naturally in moist, shady places in the coast ranges and the foothills of the Sierra, it would go well in a woodland setting. Crushed foliage has an unpleasant odor.

T. speciosissimum. (*T. flavum glaucum*). Somewhere between the above two species in size and habit, this plant is reputed to be excellent for cutting. The fluffy flower heads are lemon-yellow above tall, blue-green foliage. Two other species with yellow flowers but with less attractive, ordinary green foliage are *T. lucidum* and *T. flavum*, both 4 to 5 ft. in height.

E.C.G.

THYMUS. *Lamiaceae. (Labiatae).* THYME. Well known for its culinary value, thyme also has a number of species which are decorative and which may be planted for several garden purposes, edgings, ground covers, slope fillers, and container plants. Those described here are useful for their appearance alone. Those which form a mat make a carpet delightful to walk on. They are also good as patches in a rock garden or along the edge of borders to brush for the scent. In paths, plant as a carpet with random stones. They flourish in the chinks of stone walls. Thymes are easily propagated by division. Quite small pieces can be cut and rooted for increasing the width of a carpet. Plants can also be grown from seed, but since they hybridize freely, seedlings are apt to have mixed parentage.

T. caespititius. Native to the Iberian Peninsula, the Azores, and Madeira, this species is quite at home here on the Peninsula. It forms a mat with prostrate stems, leafy and hairy, to 2-1/2 in. tall. The leaves are hairless except along the margins, linear to oblanceolate, 1/3 in. long. The pale lilac flowers bloom in loose clusters, though somewhat sparsely.

T. x citriodorus. LEMON THYME. This cross between *T. pulegiodes* and *T. vulgaris* is a most attractive hybrid. Two selections often grown are 'Silver Queen' and 'Aureus'. The common name is derived from the scent of the foliage, though the name is applied loosely to several other species and cultivars.

T. hirsutus. As the name implies, this species is quite hairy, both stems and leaves having hairs. The stems are erect to 3 in. The leaves are stalkless, linear with edges rolled under, appearing fringed. The tiny flowers are lilac in 1/2 in. clusters.

T. praecox. MOTHER OF THYME, CREEPING THYME. This mat- forming species grows no more than 5 in. high, usually less. It is a good choice to plant between stones in a path where the crushed leaves give off a delightful fragrance. Two varieties offer a choice of flower color, 'Albus', white, or 'Coccineus', crimson. These two low forms are available in the market place, though not always under the correct name.

T. pseudolanuginosus. WOOLLY THYME. The stems are hairy only on two sides, but the leaves are densely hairy, whence the common name. A distinction from the other species is that the flowers are not in head-like clusters. This is the grayest thyme, spreading slowly to make a wide, low mat, nice to stroke.

T. vulgaris. COMMON THYME. This is the thyme most used in cooking. There are two excellent forms, 'Argenteus' and 'Aureus', the names describing the variegation. Both grow to 8 in. or more with erect, wiry, woody stems, forming dense sub-shrubs. The linear leaves are 1/4 to 1/2 in. long and more or less clustered. The edges are rolled under. When grown in a 10 in. fern pot, stems will spill over the edge and cascade. Pruning will assist this form and will be needed to keep the shrublet clean of dead wood. Sun assists good growth, but part shade is satisfactory. This thyme can even be grown in pots on the kitchen window-sill where sprigs can be used in cooking until the small plant has become so denuded that it must be replaced.

E.B.

TIARELLA. *Saxifragaceae.* FOAM FLOWER, FALSE MITREWORT. There are about six species, all but one from North America. The name is a latinized diminutive of the Greek for 'tiara', a turban-like head-dress, and alludes to the shape of the fruits. In nature they grow in damp woodlands or along stream banks and in the garden want a damp, shady location. Although called herbaceous, the leaves are persistent here in the Bay Area, and the plants are mostly hardy. The leaves are basal and spring from miniature rhizomes or stolons, which can be divided. Propagation is also by seed, when available, but the genus pollenizes readily, so the offspring may have variations.

T. wherryi. Growing in compact clumps, this densely-leafed species makes a plant about 10 in. across and 1 ft. tall when in flower. The leaves are heart-shaped, three-lobed, over 3 in. across. They are blotched at the base and turn red in the fall. Bloom is in summer, and the white flowers are in dense, erect, branchless racemes 6 to 12 to a plant. These have a foamy look, accentuated by the 10 prominent stamens in each small flower. The plants look well with ferns, cyclamen, and aquilegia. This species is from the Appalachian Mountains. It is a long-lived, well-behaved subject for the shady garden.

E.B.

TRACHELIUM caeruleum. *Campanulaceae.* THROATWORT. This plant comes from the western and central Mediterranean region. It has been an interesting addition to my garden, since I never know where it will appear next. It seeds all around, and in the better locations, I have let the seedlings remain. Some would call it a pest, I'm sure.

The plant forms clumps to 4 ft. tall. The foliage is dark green, thicker at the base of the plant, but also appearing on the wine-red stems which support flower clusters 4 to 5 in. across. The flowers are individually very tiny, ranging through shades of lavender and blue and blooming spring into fall. The look is airy and attractive. The foliage turns a handsome bronzy color in the autumn. Although these plants winter over, the new seedlings always have a more vigorous look and produce more blooms. The plant seems very adaptable to sun or shade and gets average water in my garden.

Plants to combine with it in the landscape are *Penstemon* 'Midnight', *Teucrium fruticans, Viburnum davidii* (in shadier conditions), and *Cerastium tomentosum* for an edging. This grouping will need plenty of room to perform.

M.K.

TRICYRTIS hirta. *Liliaceae.* TOAD LILY. Tricyrtis is a subtle, yet elegant, woodland perennial from Japan. It is 1-1/2 to 2-l/2 ft. tall and slowly spreads to form a beautiful lush mass of foliage. In fact, the foliage is a great asset to the plant in that the leaves are variously splotched and spattered with purple. The purple coloring fades with age, and by September or October, when the plant blooms, the leaves are a nearly uniform pale green. The flowers are a study in camouflage; they are white suffused with pale purple with a liberal supply of purple spots and blotches and seem to fade into their surroundings with ease. They are fascinating to look at close up.

Because it is such a quiet plant, it must be located at the front of the perennial border or woodland bed. An ideal spot would be at the edge of a bottom step of a short stairway in dappled shade, or at the base of a large deciduous tree.

Toad lilies require regular watering, good, loose, rich loam in shade, though not deep, dark shade. This perennial is herbaceous and is vulnerable to the predation of snails and slugs as it sprouts in February or March. Bait.

B.O'B.

TULBAGHIA. *Amaryllidaceae.* Tulbaghia is a genus of tuberous or cormous perennials native to tropical and South Africa. Their fleshy, strap-shaped leaves make a clump above which the flowering stems arise, similar to the growth habit of agapanthus, to which they are related. The flowers are borne in an umbel, the individual flowers tubular, flaring at the end into a six-petalled star. In mild winters they may stay green, but the tops are not really hardy. This winter at 27°F all the tulbaghias in my garden were cut down by frost; however, I am confident that they will re-sprout.

    T. fragrans. SWEET GARLIC. The fragrant, pinky-lavender flowers and the stems and leaves are free of the onion odor characteristic of *T. violacea.* The leaves are wider than that species, the basal clump about one foot high with the flowering stem up to 18 in. There are many flowers per umbel, although it seems not to be very free flowering. This may be because, being geographically confused by being in the northern hemisphere, it tries to bloom in winter when conditions are unsuitable. It is often grown in greenhouses as a pot plant because it is frost sensitive.

    T. violacea. SOCIETY GARLIC. The species most often grown in gardens, it has been popular for many years because of its dependability. The clumps are 1 ft. high by 1 ft. wide under a starburst of violet flowers. It blooms throughout summer and fall. It does best in full sun with regular watering and good soil, but established clumps can take tougher conditions when necessary. Snails don't mind the onion odor of the foliage, so these pests need to be guarded against. A variegated cultivar called 'Silver Lace' is smaller and less vigorous than the species but daintier and very attractive. Propagation is by division.

E.C.G.

VANCOUVERIA. *Berberidaceae.* Vancouverias are among the most primitive of the flowering plants found in our gardens. The family includes the familiar *Mahonia* and *Berberis.* Vancouverias are closely related to the epimediums and were even included in that genus when they were originally described. Like the epimediums, vancouverias are primarily grown for their elegant foliage; the flowers are an airy extra. This genus includes just three species, native to California and Oregon. The two available ones are described here. Vancouverias are easy to grow if their preferences for abundant shade, moisture, and humus are met. They bloom in May and June. The plants range in height from 6 in. to 2 ft.; the differences in height are mostly related to the amount of sun that the plants receive. These plants, again like the epimediums, will thrive among established tree roots and are often recommended as groundcovers

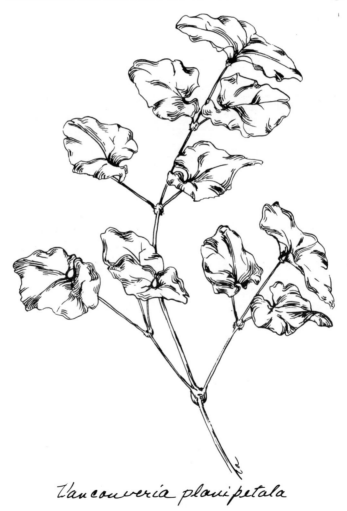

Vancouveria planipetala

under rhododendrons and azaleas. The genus was named for Captain George Vancouver, who explored much of the Pacific Northwest in the late 1700's.

V. planipetala. INSIDE-OUT FLOWER, REDWOOD IVY. Beautiful evergreen rosettes of shiny, dark green, compound leaves on black stems make this one of our most beautiful native plants for a low groundcover in the shade. The foliage is strongly reminiscent of the maidenhair ferns (*Adiantum* sp.), although the individual leaflets of this vancouveria are much larger. The plants spread slowly by rhizomes to form broad colonies when they are happily situated. The tiny white flowers are held in delicate panicles and appear to have been turned inside-out. This plant combines beautifully with other shade-loving native groundcovers such as *Oxalis oregana, Dicentra formosa,* trilliums, and ferns, especially the adiantums. Native to the Santa Cruz Mountains and ranging from the Santa Lucia Mountains of Monterey County to southern Oregon, it is usually found growing in redwood groves, which leads to one of its common names — redwood ivy.

V. hexandra. INSIDE-OUT FLOWER. This briefly deciduous (usually in early fall) perennial is very tolerant of deep shade. The small apple-green leaflets are not shiny and strongly resemble fern fronds, so much so that they may become lost if planted with maidenhair ferns. The white flowers are larger than those of *V. planipetala*, but are still small. Ranging from Mendocino County to Washington state, this species is most often found in coniferous forests. The foliage is of a much finer texture than *V. planipetala*, but I have found it to be less satisfactory as a garden plant, though more useful in very dense shade. It will not tolerate sun in our area, unlike *V. planipetala*, which will accept some light sun.

B.O'B.

Verbascum chaixii

VERBASCUM.

Scrophulariaceae. MULLEIN. A familiar sight along country roads is the common mullein, *V. thapsus,* 3 to 6 ft. tall, with a great mat of woolly basal leaves from which rise tall, leafy stalks topped by yellow-flowered spikes that seem to bloom randomly along their length. It is too large and coarse for most gardens and too prolific a self-seeder, but other members of the genus are more refined and are valuable in the perennial border as vertical accents among mounding plants. Verbascums all have in common the basal rosette of leaves from which the flowering stalk ascends; flowers borne in a spike; and, unusually for this family, a dish-shaped flower whose five petals are nearly equal. They all like well-drained soil in full sun.

V. chaixii. Over the years this species increases in vigor and sturdiness, eventually forming an erect clump 3 or more ft. in height. The basal rosette elongates into leafy stems topped with branching flower spikes. The flowers are typically yellow with a purple "eye", but there is also a white form, 'Album', also with the purple central color spot that very effectively complements other purple flowers nearby. The "eye" is actually a brush of purple hairs on the stamens.

V. phoeniceum. PURPLE MULLEIN. This plant is usually seen in one of its many hybrid forms that have extended the color range from the original soft purple to pink, white, and salmon, all somewhat muted and harmonious together. I have never seen it attain the 4 or 5 ft. height that *Hortus Third* says it is capable of; in fact, the stems are disappointingly lax and nearly always need staking. Nor does it appear to be reliably perennial. But it is a willing bloomer, comes easily from seed, and the colors have a special appeal that insures its welcome in the garden.

E.C.G.

VERBENA. *Verbenaceae.* VERVAIN.

V. lilacina. A beautiful workhorse in the garden, *V. lilacina* is rarely out of flower. The much divided foliage is gray-green and produces a light effect in the border. The lavender-purple flowers have white centers and are borne in clusters. As these fade, be sure to remove them to keep the plant looking its best. Grow it in full sun with good drainage for heavier bloom. This plant is from Baja California, yet it seems perfectly happy growing in our colder, wetter climate.

V. peruviana. From Argentina and Brazil comes this candidate for a hot, dry spot in the garden. It is much more common in southern California than around the Bay Area, but if you have a sunny hillside or corner that gets little water and that you would like to forget, this is a plant worth trying. This commonly planted species spreads rapidly and has a profusion of vivid scarlet, flat-topped blooms rising 4 to 6 in. above flat, gray-green foliage. There are hybrids which spread more slowly and come in a variety of colors. Mildew on the foliage can be a problem; deep, infrequent waterings are suggested, as well as good air circulation.

V. rigida. This truly hardy perennial is native to southern Brazil and Argentina and has become naturalized in the U.S. along the southeastern coast to Texas. It is so often planted in beds and street plantings that it is almost a cliche. That doesn't make it a plant to overlook, however. It is much more reliably hardy than *V. peruviana*, and its lavender blossoms on 1 to 2 ft. tall stems backed by dark green leaves can do wonders for a difficult spot. It is drought tolerant and grows in almost any well-drained soil. Mildew develops if water is on the leaves too long. It blooms from seed in its first season.

V. tenuisecta. MOSS VERBENA. Another South American species, this one is now naturalized from Georgia to Louisiana. It is quite different from its relatives because of its finely cut, dark green leaves. These form a mound, handsome even when not in bloom. Its flower stems grow upright or horizontally, and the flowers, a nice lavender, are distributed along the stem rather than in a head. The flower stems should be cut back after the first flush of bloom, or the center will get bare. Some of the stems are procumbent, and if you leave them, they will root. I have had good luck replanting those rooted stems.

This plant was suggested to me as a good one for a drought tolerant garden, and it was an admirable suggestion, but like other verbenas, it wants some water. It grows best in lots of sun, and in my experience, does not suffer from mildew as much as the others, another point in its favor. A cultivar, 'Alba', is listed, which should be lovely, backed by the dark foliage.

M.G.
B.O'B.

Verbena tenuisecta
Verbena lilacina

ZAUSCHNERIA. *Onagraceae.* CALIFORNIA FUCHSIA, HUMMINGBIRD FLOWER. Our California fuchsias (botanically not fuchsias at all, though of the same family) are a useful addition to any garden. They come in several sizes and habits and are quite adaptable. Though in the wild we find them growing in a lean, fast-draining soil with little water, this native adapts quickly and produces lush foliage and larger flowers given regular garden irrigation and a compost-amended soil. Tall varieties should be severely pruned after the blossoms finish. After pruning in November the plants will be barely noticeable until new growth appears in February.

These perennials are easily grown from seed sown in a finely screened soil, cuttings, or root division. The larger forms spread by underground runners and consideration of this trait must be given when selecting a planting site. Many of our native plant nurseries and local chapters of the California Native Plant Society have zauschnerias for sale. Most readily available are *Z. californica* and a cultivar named 'U. C. Hybrid'.

Zauschneria makes a splendid show with our native penstemons, shrubby mimulus and *Monardella* in a small border situation. Adding California fuchsias to the dry native bulb bed lends color long after the bulbs have finished. In a larger site, its foliage and flowers stand out against low-growing *Ceanothus gloriosus* and taller *Ribes speciosum*.

Z. californica. This standby is a dependable bloomer from July through October with a color range from orange to deep red. A pink form called 'Solidarity Pink' was recently introduced, and the low, white-flowering form called 'Alba' has been on the market for some years. The 1 to 2 in. tubular flowers are a favorite of hummingbirds. The plants will grow to 2 ft. high and some are rampant runners. There are several sub-species with varying habits. Some of these plants will turn up in nurseries as separate species and they do range considerably in size. *Z. c. latifolia* forms mats 3 to 6 in. high and disappears in winter.

Z. cana. The leaves are quite narrow and silvery green. 'Hurricane Point' forms tidy clumps 6 in. high by 1 ft. wide and is evergreen in our mild climate.

B. Coe

COMMON NAMES INDEX

Common name	Scientific name
	(Numerals refer to page numbers.)

Alpine Geranium	*Erodium chamaedriodes*, **40**
Alumroot	*Heuchera*, **60**
American Alumroot	*Heuchera americana*, **60**
Baby's Breath	*Gypsophila paniculata*, **50**
Balloon Flower	*Platycodon grandiflora*, **84**
Beach Wallflower	*Erysimum concinnum*, **44**
Beach Wormwood	*Artemisia stellerana*,**14**
Beard Tongue	*Penstemon*, **80**
Bishop's Hat	*Epimedium grandiflorum*, **37**
Bleeding Heart	*Dicentra spectabile*, **33**
Bush Germander	*Teucrium fruticans*, **104**
Buttercup	*Ranunculus*, **86**
Butterfly Weed	*Asclepias*, **15**
California Fuchsia	*Zauchneria californica*, **117**
Campion	*Silene*, **100**
Candle Larkspur	*Delphinium elatum*, **29**
Candytuft	*Iberis*, **64**
Carpet Bugle	*Ajuga*, **2**
Catmint	*Nepeta* X *faassenii*, **74**
Catnip	*Nepeta cataria*, **74**
Chainlink Artemisia	*Artemisia canescens*, **12**
Checkerbloom	*Sidalcea malvaeflora*, **99**
Christmas Rose	*Helleborus niger*, **55**
Cinquefoil	*Potentilla*, **84**
Columbine	*Aquilegia*, **6**
Common Bleeding Heart	*Dicentra spectabile*, **34**
Common Thyme	*Thymus vulgaris*, **108**
Coral Bells	*Heuchera sanguinea*, **61**
Corsican Hellebore	*Helleborus argutifolius*, **55**
Cranesbill	*Geranium*, **48**
Creeping Buttercup	*Ranunculus repens*, **86**
Creeping Thyme	*Thymus praecox*, **108**
Curry Plant	*Helichrysum angustifolium*, **53**
Daylily	*Hemerocallis*, **57**

Common Name	Scientific Name
Dead Nettle	*Lamium maculatum*, **67**
Dittany of Crete	*Origanum dictamnus*, **78**
Dune Sage	*Artemisia pycnocephala*, **12**
Dusty Miller	*Artemisia arborescens*, **11**
Dusty Miller	*Centaurea cineraria*, **25**
Dusty Miller	*Senecio cineraria*, **98**
English Lavendar	*Lavendula angustifolia*, **67**
European Pasque Flower	*Anemone pulsatilla*, **4**
Evening Primrose	*Oenothera hookeri*, **76**
Fairy Fan Flower	*Scaevola* 'Mauve Clusters', **97**
False Dragonhead	*Physostegia virginiana*, **83**
False Heather	*Cuphea hyssopifolia*, **28**
False Mitrewort	*Tiarella wherryi*, **109**
False Solomon's Seal	*Smilacina*, **101**
Fernleaf Yarrow	*Achillea filipendulina*, **1**
Fleabane	*Erigeron karvinskianus*, **39**
Foam Flower	*Tiarella wherryi*, **109**
Foxglove	*Digitalis* X *mertonensis*, **35**
French Lavender	*Lavendula dentata*, **68**
French Tarragon	*Artemisia dracunculus*, **12**
Fried Egg Plant	*Romney coulteri*, **88**
Fringed Bleeding Heart	*Dicentra exima*, **34**
Fringed Wormwood	*Artemisia frigida*, **12**
Gentian Sage	*Salvia patens*, **94**
Germander	*Teucrium*, **104**
Globe Thistle	*Echinops exaltatus*, **36**
Golden Eardrops	*Dicentra chrysantha*, **34**
Heliotrope	*Heliotropus arborescens*, **54**
Herb-of-Grace	*Ruta graveolens*, **91**
Heron's Bill	*Erodium*, **40**
Hummingbird Flower	*Zauchneria californica*, **117**
Inside-out Flower	*Vancouveria planipetala*, **113**
Island Alumroot	*Heuchera maxima*, **61**
Island Shooting Star	*Dodecatheon clevelandii*, **35**
Japanese Anemone	*Anemone* X *hybrida*, **5**

Common Name	Scientific Name
Jerusalem Sage	*Phlomis fruticosa*, **82**
Kahili Ginger	*Hedychium gardneranum*, **51**
Kangaroo Paw	*Anigozanthus*, **5**
Lady-in-a-Bath	*Dicentra spectabile*, **34**
Lamb's Ears	*Stachys byzantina*, **102**
Larkspur	*Delphinium*, **29**
Lavender	*Lavendula*, **67**
Lavender Cotton	*Santolina chamaecyparissus*, **95**
Lemon Thyme	*Thymus* X *citriodorus*, **108**
Lenten Rose	*Helleborus orientalis*, **57**
Leopard Plant	*Ligularia tussilaginea*, 'Aureo-maculata', **70**
Lion's Ear	*Leonotis leonurus*, **69**
Lion's Tail	*Leonotis leonurus*, **69**
Maiden Pink	*Dianthus deltoides*, **31**
Maiden's Wreath	*Francoa ramosa*, **47**
Matilija poppy	*Romneya coulteri*, **88**
Meadow Rue	*Thalictrum*, **105**
Mexican Evening Primrose	*Oenothera berlandieri*, **76**
Mexican Tulip Poppy	*Hunnemania fumariifolia*, **62**
Milfoil	*Achillea millefolium*, **1**
Milkweed	*Asclepias*, **15**
Monkey Flower	*Mimulus*, **72**
Moss Verbena	*Verbena tenuisecta*, **116**
Mother-of-Thyme	*Thymus praecox*, **108**
Mullein	*Verbascum*, **114**
Mullein Pink	*Lychnis coronaria*, **71**
Obedience Plant	*Physostegia virginiana*, **83**
Old Woman	*Artemisia stellerana*, **14**
Oregano	*Origanum*, **78**
Perennial Larkspur	*Delphinium elatum*, **29**
Pitcher Sage	*Salvia spathacea*, **95**
Plume Poppy	*Macleaya cordata*, **72**
Point Reyes Wallflower	*Erysimum concinnum*, **44**
Poker Plant	*Kniphofia uvaria*, **66**
Poppy Flowered Anemone	*Anemone coronaria*, **4**

Common Name	Scientific Name
Purple Mullein	*Verbascum phoeniceum*, 115
Red Buckwheat	*Eriogonum grande rubescens*, 39
Red Hot Poker	*Kniphofia uvaria*, 66
Redwood Ivy	*Vancouveria planipetala*, 113
Rock Cress	*Arabis*, 8
Rock Geranium	*Heuchera americana*, 60
Rock Jasmine	*Androsace*, 3
Rocky Mountain Columine	*Aquilegia caerulea*, 6
Rosemary	*Rosmarinus*, 88
Rue	*Ruta graveolens*, 91
Russian Sage	*Perovskia atriplicifolia*, 82
Saffron Buckwheat	*Eriogonum crocatum*, 40
Sage	*Salvia*, 92
Sandhill Sage	*Artemisia pycnocephala*, 13
Sandwort	*Arenaria*, 10
Savory	*Satureja*, 97
Sea Lavender	*Limonium perezii*, 70
Seaside Daisy	*Erigeron glaucus*, 38
Shasta Daisy	*Chrysantheum maximum*, 26
Shooting Star	*Dodecatheon clevelandii*, 35
Siberian Bugloss	*Brunnera macrophylla*, 20
Siberian Wallflower	*Erysimum heiraciifolium*, 43
Slipperwort	*Calceolaria integrifolia*, 22
Snow-in-Summer	*Cerastium tomentosum*, 25
Soapwort	*Saponaria ocymoides*, 96
Society Garlic	*Tulbaghia violacea*, 111
Spanish Lavender	*Lavendula stoechas*, 68
Spurge	*Euphorbia*, 44
Statice	*Limonium perezii*, 70
Stokes Aster	*Stokesia laevis*, 103
Stonecrop	*Sedum*, 99
Sun Rose	*Helianthemum nummularium*, 52
Sundrops	*Oenothera perennis*, 77
Swamp Sunflower	*Helianthus angustifolius*, 52
Sweet Garlic	*Tulbaghia fragrans*, 111
Tarragon	*Artemisia dracunculus*, 12
Throatwort	*Trachelium caeruleum*, 110

Common Name	Scientific Name
Thyme	*Thymus*, **108**
Toad Lily	*Tricyrtis hirta*, **110**
Tree germander	*Teucrium fruticans*, **104**
Tree Poppy	*Romneya coulteri*, **88**
Tussock Harebell	*Campanula carpatica*, **22**
Twinspur	*Diascia barberae*, **32**
Vervain	*Verbena*, **115**
Wall Germander	*Teucrium chamaedrys*, **104**
Wall Rock Cress	*Arabis caucasica*, **9**
Wallflower	*Erysimum*, **42**
Western Bleeding Heart	*Dicentra formosa*, **34**
Western Columbine	*Aquilegia formosa*, **6**
Wild Buckwheat	*Erigeron*, **38**
Wild Ginger	*Asarum caudatum*, **14**
Wild Marjorum	*Origanum vulgare*, **79**
Wind Flower	*Anemone*, **4**
Winter Savory	*Satureja montana*, **97**
Wood Sage	*Teucrium scorodonia*, **105**
Wood Spurge	*Euphorbia amygdaloides*, **44**
Woolly Thyme	*Thymus pseudolanuginosa*, **108**
Wormwood	*Artemisia absinthium*, **11**
Yarrow	*Achillea*, **1**

CONTRIBUTORS

Debbie Armstrong, Palo Alto	*D. A.*
Susan Beall, Palo Alto	*S. B.*
Keith Bickford, Los Altos	*K. B.*
Emily Brown, Hillsborough	*E. B.*
Ed Carman, Los Gatos	*E. C.*
Betsy Clebsch, La Honda	*B. C.*
Barbara Coe, Morgan Hill	*B. Coe*
Mabel Crittenden, Portola Valley	*M. C.*
Daphne Dorney, Los Altos	*D. D.*
Maggie Gage, Stanford	*M. G.*
Elizabeth C. Garbett, Los Altos Hills	*E. C. G.*
Mary Kaye, Los Altos	*M. K.*
Ted Kipping, San Francisco	*T. K.*
Bart O'Brien, Woodside	*B. O'B.*
Allicin Rauzin, Palo Alto	*A. R.*
Page Sanders, Palo Alto	*P. S.*
Claire Steede, Redwood City	*C. S.*
Marilou Vivanco, Palo Alto	*M. V.*
Betty Young, Redwood City	*B. Y.*